COWBOY SLANG

by

Edgar R. "Frosty" Potter

Illustrated by Ron Scofield

Golden West Publishers

Library of Congress Cataloging-in-Publication Data

Potter, Edgar R.
  Cowboy slang.

  1. Cowboys--Language (New words, slang, etc.)--
Dictionaries. 2. English language--Slang--Dictionaries.
3. English language--West (U.S.)--Slang--Dictionaries.
4. Americanisms--West (U.S.)--Dictionaries. 5. Cattle
brands. 6. Earmarks. I. Title.
PE3727.C6P6 1985   427'.0088636   85-24930
ISBN 0-914846-21-3 (pbk.)

Printed in the United States of America

Golden West Publishers
4113 N. Longview Ave.
Phoenix, AZ 85014, USA

DEDICATION

In memory of my son
Gordon R. Potter
and my wife Anne C. Potter

CONTENTS

PREFACE

I've been lookin' at quite a few books lately and I find that most books have got what is called a PREFACE up towards the front end. I looked it up and found that it means "a start," and that's exactly what I want to do right now, start.

Of course, the trouble with a PREFACE is that if you make it too long, some tight-fisted folks will read the PREFACE and find out all about the book and then not buy it. I've seen lots of folks stand in a corner and do just that, and when they get it read, they will sheepishly head for the door.

First, I want you readers to know that these cowboy slang phrases are not just for readin' purposes. If you study them you'll soon learn to TALK like a cowboy. There has already been over 10,000 of these COWBOY SLANG books sold, but a lot of folks said they would like to have more of the slang phrases. So, in order to please these folks, I got busy and dug up near another thousand of them making all told close on to 2,000 which aught to satisfy most everybody.

I remember once readin' about an old feller who claimed "a single picture is worth a thousand words." Why, that old fossil don't know what he's talkin' about. You can take most any of my cowboy slang phrases, set back in yore chair "as calm as a skunk in the moonlight," close yore eyes an' conjure up a word picture that will make the one picture idea about "as useless as settin' a milk bucket under a bull."

Now to show you what I mean about conjuring up a word picture. Let's take the very first Cowboy Slang phrase in my book which happens to be "man that straddles fence usually has sore crotch." All right, now let's see what kind of a word picture you can conjure up in yore mind? Me? I see a feller with a saddle slung over his back. He walks up to a bob-wire fence that he wants to get through. There's five wires all stretched fiddle-string tight and he knows darn well he couldn't crawl betwix that many tight wires without "losin' enough hide to half-sole an elephant." He stands there cogitatin'.

About that time here comes a hombre on hossback. Howdy's are exchanged and the hossback feller says "how come yore afoot Slim?"

"Hoss stepped in a badger hole an' I had to shoot 'im" said 'tother feller.

"Hmmmmmmmm, that's bad, must be all of 20 miles to yore spread, ain't it?"

"Yup, but I'll make it if I can get myself through this damned fence all in one piece."

"Hmmmmmmmm," the ridin' feller says again. "Well, how about tossin' yore saddle over the fence, then crawl up behind me an' I'll ride up as close to the fence as I can an' then yuh see if yuh can fall over it." Slim got on, and Shorty edges his skittish bronc up as close to the fence as the bronc will go an' Slim starts to ease himself over. Well, when Slim starts to ease himself over, why the bronc starts to ease himself over the other way, which leaves Slim no choice but to land a'straddle the bobwire fence.

Now that's the end of my word picture, an' it's plain easy to see how I got the Cowboy Slang phrase "man that straddles fence usually has sore crotch."

So now you can see why you should only take one Cowboy Slang phrase at a time. That way, if you think up a little story about each of the phrases, why yuh will probably have enough stuff thunk up to last maybe fourteen years or so. Let's just put down a few more phrases to give you the idea. Like,

- Tryin' to scratch his ear with his elbow.

- His hoss throwed him forked-end up.

- She didn't wear 'nough clothes to dust a fiddle.

- "Oh, is that you, ma" said the little porcupine
  as he backed into a cactus.

Now everyone of them would make a darn good word picture, don't yuh think?

Most folks will have to agree that when you read an average book, you usually have to read several pages or more of "not worth a darn" stuff before you come to something worth reading. Now that is something that I have aimed to keep away from. I claim that every solitary one of my pages will have something that you will want to read. Now don't get the idea that Cowboy Phrases are the only thing in my book, Oh no, I've loaded it with about everything I can think of that has more or less something to do with the Old West to make it interesting to read. It's not only for Pa and Ma, but is good for the entire family. And, Grandma, why don't you go up in the attic and I'll bet you four-bits you can find more than one piece of Western gear that Grandpappy used to own. If you are lucky you might find his old .45 Colt. And did you know that back around 1903 a Colt .45 used to cost $15.50? An old one like you may have is now worth from $500 to $1000.

Now, of course, when you place it on your center table to show it off to your friends, why don't be coy about it and say it's just a conversation piece when you know darn well you have already cleaned the bore and tested the action and maybe have a few cartridges stashed away in a bureau drawer where only you know where they are.

I might say though, Grandma, should you find maybe half a box of Grandpa's old .45's, there's a good chance that they are probably loaded with black powder and might a-got damp and are not too reliable. So shove 'em down a post hole and get yoreself a fresh box. But what with them costing so durned much these days maybe you could split a box with Aunt Emma or some neighbor lady.

And remember, Grandma, these are getting to be rough times, so don't let nobody take no advantage of you. Keep yore iron handy an' you'll be safe if you do like I say.

Now, I would like to say that you will be surprised at what you find in my new revised COWBOY SLANG. I can assure that you will not find much, if any, "off-color" stuff in it. I know that folks of all sizes and ages and from all walks of life will read and retain the book and I don't want them to be embarrassed at the material in it. Some books you read will near curl your hair. Well, mine won't!

"Frosty"

P.S. I see now that I have done exactly what I shouldn't a done, make the PREFACE so long that folks can just read it and won't have to buy the book. Oh well, I'll take a chance on that, as I know you will want to buy and keep the book for yourself.

COWBOY SLANG

Actions

- A man that straddles fence usually has a sore crotch.
- He started jumping up and down like a barrel boundin' down hill.
- Tryin' to scratch his ear with his elbow.
- Reelin' 'round like a pup tryin' to find a spot to lie down.
- A scratchin' like he had a shirt full of fleas.
- About as busy as a hibernating bear.
- Found him sleepin' gentle as a dead calf.
- Light an' take comfort in a frog squat.
- The come-hither nickering of an eager mare.
- He lets out a stud-horse whistle as would pull the picket pin of every filly 'round.
- Stopped to breathe his pony.
- Lets out a yell as would scare a tired work-bull off his feed ground.
- A change of pasture makes for a fatter calf.
- Nothin' to do but stand 'round an' scratch his seat.

Afraid

- He bolted like a jackrabbit in tall grass.
- Jumped like he'd stepped on a raw egg.
- Jumpin' like a speckled-legged frog from a dry lake.
- A funny feelin' was runnin' up an' down my spine.
- If I'd had bristles I'd a resembled a wild hog.
- Made his skin get up an' crawl all over him.
- It'd make the hair of a buffalo robe stand up.

Agreeable

- He took to it like a bear to a honey tree.
- Always as mild as sweet milk she was.
- He's as slow acting as wet gunpowder.

Appearance

- As bowlegged as a barrel hoop.

Man that straddles fence usually has sore crotch.

- He was all swoll up like a toad in a churn.
- Her face was as wrinkled as a burnt boot.
- As gnarled as a cedar root.
- A regular buck-nun for looks.
- Had eyes as baleful as death.

Awkward

- As awkward as a blind bear in a bramble patch.
- As clumsy as a floundered stud.
- As graceful as an elephant tryin' to use a typewriter.
- As awkward as a bull in a china closet.

Big

- He couldn't hide no more than a hill.
- Feet so big his tracks looked like where a steer had bedded down.
- When he fell in the river he dried it up for forty rods.
- Had feet as big as a loadin'-chute.
- Strong 'nough to derail a freight train.
- Could take first prize at a bull show.
- Big as a hoop on a molasses barrel.
- He was as big as a twenty-mule-team freight wagon.
- Showed up as big as a skinned hoss.
- Most big 'nough to shade an elephant.
- He must a been born full growed.
- Big 'nough to hunt bears with a switch.
- As broad beamed and cow-hocked as a Holstein's behind.
- Big as a lead-bull in a buffalo herd.
- Had a house big 'nough to bed down a night herd.
- Mexican spur rowels as big as a soup plate.
- She had cooties as big as a yearlins.

Black

- As black as midnight during a new moon.
- Blackern' a blacksmith's apron.
- As black as a spade flush.

- Blackern' a stack of stove lids.
- Black as a chuck-wagon skillet.

Blind

- As blind as a post hole.
- Blind as a snubbin' post.
- So blind he couldn't see through a bobwire fence.
- Blind as a rattler in August.

Braggart

- He had callouses from pattin' his own back.
- Bragged himself out of a place to lean agin' the bar.
- He throws too much dust.
- Was handin' out a lot of Mexican oats.
- He was just a case of big behavior.
- Always lettin' off a little steam.
- Mostly all gurgle an' no guts.
- He was as full of wind as a bull in corn time.

Brands

- Steers a wearin' brands so big yuh could read them in the moonlight.
- Yuh could've a spotted that brand through a hoss blanket.
- Wore a brand as big as a patent medicine sign.
- Hoss was branded till he looked like a walkin' brand book.
- He was checkin' the hoss's brands to see who had come to the shindig.
- Made his livin' burnin' an' trimmin' up calves.

Brave

- As gritty as aigs rolled in sand.
- Knows how to die standin' up.
- Had more guts than yuh could hang on a fence.
- Had more sand than the Sahara Desert.
- A gent with sand in his craw.
- He'll fight a rattler an' give him first bite.
- Craw jammed plumb full of sand an' fightin' tallow.

Nothin' to do but stand around and scratch his seat.

- Had plenty sand in his gizzard.
- He'll fight a buzz-saw an' give it three revolutions.

Bronc Rider

- He went sailin' off—his hind laigs kickin' in the air like a migratin' bullfrog.
- He et gravel without stoopin'.
- That hoss throwed him clean into a funeral parlor.
- There's a heap more to bein' a rider than just settin' on a hoss an' let yore feet hang down.
- Yuh got throwed so high I was lookin' to see if St. Peter had whittled his initials in yore boot soles.
- Felt like I'd been ridin' the rough string with a borrowed saddle.
- I shore was a achin' in a lot of new places.
- I was knockin' a hole in my chest with my chin.
- The sun was soon a shinin' on his moccasins.
- After three jumps he hit the ground and laid still.
- Got up with three handfuls of something he didn't want.
- All I could do was just aim to run down his mainspring.
- I was ridin' a hoss that could outbuck a bobcat with his tail afire.
- We had to pluck him of cactus-spines so he wouldn't look like a porcupine.
- He left his hoss in an unscheduled flight.
- The cantle of the saddle hit me in the caboose an' I started for a flight to Mars.
- Throwed me further than a Death Valley buzzard can smell a dry canteen.
- Thet hoss looked as easy as shootin' fish in a dry lake.
- He could stomp yuh into the ground so deep you'd take root an' sprout.
- I didn't break nothin', but all my hinges, bolts an' nuts was shore loosened.
- I got throwed so high I could've said my prayers before I lit.
- He was clawin' leather by the handfulls.
- I only wanted to go up an' see what the moon was made of.

- For a minute I thought I'd mounted backward as I shore in hell couldn't find his haid.
- I soared so high it was damn scary without wings.
- He could curry the kinks out'en a bronc's backbone.
- He stuck like a tick in a lamb's tail.
- Yuh couldn't a chopped him loose from thet hoss with an axe.
- He screwed hisself down in the saddle an' stuck like a postage stamp.
- The way he rid yuh would think he was on a hobby-horse.
- He couldn't ride nothin' wildern' a wheel-chair.
- After that ride all I needed to make me a cripple was a tin cup an' a handful of pencils.
- He couldn't even ride in a covered wagon tied to the seat.
- Thet hoss gave me a better merry-go-round ride than yuh pay a nickel for at a carnival.
- That hoss soon had 'em pickin' daisies.
- His hoss throwed him forked-end up.
- Just keep one leg on each side an' yore mind in the middle.
- That hoss grassed him in a hurry.
- Ridin' the rough string ain't like attendin' a knittin' bee.
- He can scratch hell out of anything that wears hair.
- He shore covers a lot of leather.
- He couldn't ride a rail fence in a stiff breeze.

Buckshot

- Buckshot shore leaves a mean an' oozy corpse.
- Absorb a load of buckshot an' they'll have to pick yuh up with a blotter.
- Buckshot means burying every time.

Bugs and Varmints

- He was furnishing bed an' board to a whole cavy of crawlin' homesteaders.
- So many bedbugs he could'a drove 'em down the road.
- I'd rather have greybacks than fleas anytime.
- Cooties graze an' bed down, but a flea ain't never satisfied.
- It was hard to tell which needed dippin' worse, him or his cattle.

Busted

- He eased back in his chair and got ready to slide under the table.
- He was always tryin' to keep the wolf from havin' pups on his doorstep.

Busy

- Busy as a kid pulling out a sliver.
- As busy as a little dog in tall oats.
- Busy as a one-armed paper hanger.
- Busiern' a hen drinking out of a pan.
- Busy as a brockle-faced dogie in flytime.
- Busier than a one-armed monkey at a flea festival.
- As busy as a tumbleweed in a mule track.
- Busiern' a one-armed man saddlin' a green bronc.
- Busy as a prairie dog after a gully washer.
- Busy as a chambermaid in a livery stable.

Calm

- As cool as a skunk in the moonlight.
- Calm as a horse-trough.
- Things got quietern' a hole in the ground.
- Settin' as calm as a toad in the sun.

Camp Cook

- Cussin' a range cook is as risky as brandin' a mule's tail.
- Best damn cook as ever throwed dish-water under a chuck wagon.
- He jest bogged down a couple a raisins an' called it a puddin'.

Campfire

- He wore out three hats a tryin' to get the damn'd cow-pies a burnin'.

Cautious

- So cautious he would ride a mile to spit.
- He was always as aloof as a mountain goat.

Chance

- Had as much chance as a grasshopper in an anthill.
- As much chance as a rabbit in a hound's mouth.
- No more chance than a short-tailed bull in fly time.
- As much chance as a one-legged man at a kickin' contest.
- He just blowed in with the tumbleweeds.
- No more chance than a hen at a mass meeting of coyotes.

Clean

- Bright and clean as a new mirror.
- After he comes out of the dippin' vat an' buys everything the barbers got, his own folks don't know him by sight or smell.
- So clean and brown he looked like he'd been scrubbed with saddle soap.
- Makin' lather with laundry soap an' alkali water is like tryin' to find a hoss thief in heaven.
- He stood in front of a busted mirror a tryin' to divorce his whiskers.
- His shavin' was mostly delappin' an' wattlin' till he looked like he'd had an argument with a catamount.
- His primpin' was shore hard on the soap supply an' stock water.
- He stood naked by the water tank a washin' out the canyon.

Cold

- Coldern' a Montana welldriller.
- As cold as a witch's caress.
- So cold the cows gave icicles.
- Cold 'nough to make a polar bear hunt cover.
- Coldern' a knot on the North Pole.
- Colder than hell on a stoker's holiday.
- Coldern' a pawnbroker's smile.
- He was as blue as a whetstone.
- As cold as a dead snake.
- Shakin' like a chihuahua pup with a chill.
- Coldern' frog legs.
- Shiverin' like a lizard lookin' for a hot rock.
- Colder than a mother-in-law's kiss.

As bow legged as a barrel hoop.

Complaining

- Kickin' never gets yuh nowheres lessen yore a mule.

Conceited

- He's as full of conceit as a barber's cat.
- One of them fellars as thinks the sun comes up specifically to hear him crow.
- As conceited as a flea full of blood.
- His head's all swoll up big as a kraut barrel.

Contented

- Purrin' like a kitten in a creamery.
- As happy as a fly in a currant pie.

Courting

- He soon had her tied to the snortin' post.
- Trapped hisself a squaw.
- She soon had him cinched to the last hole.
- Had his tail over the dashboard an' was a rarin' to go.
- Range calico was as scarce as sunflowers on a Christmas tree.
- Come a purty gal an' the whole range would be sufferin' Cupid's cramps.
- He called on her as regular as a goose goes barefooted.
- She-stuff can shore make a pealer get his spurs tangled.
- Thet little feller with a bow an' arrer can shore bugger up a cowboy.
- He'd spent his wages on pies an' throat-ticklin' stuff in order to chin with the purty hash-slinger.
- Yuh can't hitch up a horse with a coyote.
- He did hisself some heavy courtin'.
- After she caught him he was plumb lady-broke.
- He got hisself a mail-order wife.

Coward

- He bellered like a fresh-cut bull.
- He was all gurgle an' no guts.
- Had a yellow streak down his back so wide it lapped plumb 'round to his briskit bone.

- As yeller as mustard without the bite.
- He shore had cold feet for such a hot country.
- He was as gun-shy as a female institute.
- About as harmless as a pet rabbit.
- Jumped like a scorpin had fell down his neck.
- As afraid as a green bronc in a thunderstorm.
- Mister, go hunt up somethin' yuh can use for a backbone.
- His guts were as slack as fiddle strings.
- Had no more guts than a snake has hips.
- A few lightnin' bugs would make him run til his tongue hung out a foot and forty inches.
- As scart as a rabbit in a wolf's mouth.
- He was paper-backed an' full of butter.
- He ran his boot-heels over sidestepping trouble.
- He was shakin' like a willow in the wind.
- It didn't take much of a jag of lead to make him hit the trail.
- His eyes bulged out like a tromped-on toad.

Cowtowns (Tough)

- Yuh couldn't hold me in thet town with a Spanish bit.
- A bad place to be an' have yore gun stick.
- A town where most doors swing both ways.
- Where the dance-hall gals bare more hide to the evenin' breeze than an Indian in a breech-clout.
- A town of sun, sand an' blisters.
- They called the hotel fellers bellhops. I didn't see no bells, but I shore made 'em hop.
- A town where the undertaker was the most prosperous feller in it.
- The town was so tough all the hoot-owls sang bass.

Crazy

- As crazy as popcorn on a hot skillet.
- Somebody done stole his rudder.
- Knockin' 'round like a blind dog in a meat market.
- I rekkon the heat kinda addled his think box.
- He was fullgrown in body only.

- As crazy as a parrot eatin' stick candy.
- He was plumb weak north of his ears.
- He was spinnin' 'round like a button on a privy door.
- Crazier'n a locoed bedbug.
- As crazy as a sheepherder.
- He didn't even know where to scratch a hog.
- So narrow-minded he could look through a keyhole with both eyes at the same time.
- Kind of off his mental reservation.
- Crazy as a woman's watch.
- His memory was as dim as the old buffalo trails.
- His intelligence shore ain't in camp.
- If'n yuh bored a hole in his haid yuh wouldn't find 'nough brains to grease a skillet.
- He couldn't sell hack-saw blades in a hoosegow.
- He's now studyin' to be a half-wit.
- So nutty he couldn't see through a ladder.
- When the Lord poured in his brains somebody musta jaggled His arm.

Crooked

- As crooked as a snake in a cactus patch.
- The trail was crookeder'n a privy door latch.
- He's so crooked his hair is kinky.
- So crooked a rattler'd break his back a trailin' him.
- Crooked 'nough to sleep on a corkscrew.
- He's so crooked he has to screw on his socks.
- So crooked he could sleep in the shade of a posthole auger.
- So crooked he could eat nails an' spit out corkscrews.

Dancing

- Dancing in them days wasn't just wigglin' 'round an' shakin' yore rump.
- He shore was a makin' the calico crack.
- Men were cussin' their blisters an' the boots as made them.
- Gents didn't miss a dance even if their feet were on fire.
- He soon had her long dress a poppin' like crackin' the whip.

- Feet feelin' like they had wintered on a hard pasture.
- The caller was a man with leather lungs an' a loud mouth an' had his head reared back like a coffee-pot lid.
- He was shore makin' that fiddle talk a language to put ginger in yore feet.

Dark

- Dark as midnight under a skillet.
- So dark all the bats stayed home.
- So dark yuh couldn't find yore nose with both hands.
- Dark as the insides of a black bear.
- It was as dark as a lobo's cave.
- Dark 'nough to slow down a bat.
- So damn dark yuh could feel it.

Danger

- As dangerous as standin' bare-assed in a nest of rattlers.
- Crossin' that killer's about as dangerous as walkin' in quicksand over hell.
- When I see the fix I'm in I starts a askin' old Saint Pete for a passport.
- About as dangerous as bein' up the same tree with a grizzly.
- To ride through that brush a man needed one of them suits made by a blacksmith.

Dead

- He saddled a cloud an' rode to the great beyond.
- He was starin' at the sky an' seein' nothin'.
- Dead as a can of corned beef.
- Boothill is full of them fellers who pulled their triggers without aiming.
- He was caught short an' now he's deadern' hell in some preacher's back yard.
- The grass is now wavin' over him.
- He got a pill in the stomach he couldn't digest.
- We put him to bed with a pick an' shovel.
- I made 'em deadern a beaver hat.

Dirty

- As dirty as a flop-eared hound.

**Lived in the desert so long he knowed
all the lizards by their front names.**

- Looks like he's plumb water shy.
- Smell so thick in his cabin the candles were ashamed to burn.

Dress

- He sloshes his hat at a jack-duce angle over his off ear.
- She was as naked as a brandin' iron.
- Felt as important as a pup with a new collar.
- He was all ragged out in his fancy doodads.
- Had on an outfit that was shore flasharaity.
- Always a ridin' an illustrated saddle with pictures on it an' spent his time a lookin' at his shadow.
- All the boys were gopherin' through their warbags to drag out their wrinkled low-neck clothes for the shindig.
- He goes swallow-forkin' to town in his full war paint.
- Dressed as cocky as the king of spades.
- Always dressed up like a sore wrist.
- He looked like a dime novel on a spree.
- Had on one of them black suits what with no front an' just a little windbreak down the back.
- He ain't a cowboy if his shirt-tail is at half mast.
- When he goes courtin' he lets his spurs out to the town hole.
- Them gals shore looked temptin' what with their freshed-up spit-curls an' chalked noses.
- Folks on his mother's side wore moccasins.
- She displayed a splendor that'd make a peacock go into the discard.
- Had on boots so fine yuh could see the wrinkles in his socks.
- Looked as ragged as a sheepherder's britches.
- So civilized he toted a bumbershoot an' wore galluses.
- His stiff collar was so high he had to mount a soap box to spit.
- She didn't have on 'nough clothes to dust a fiddle.
- His patent leather hair was slickern' a Shewahwah pup's.
- All spraddled out in his low-necked clothes.
- Gals in them days didn't show much of their fetlocks.
- So duded up he showed up public as a zebra.
- He looked like a ridin' advertisement for a leather shop.

- When the missus makes me wear a tie, I feel like I'm tied to a post.
- He was always puttin' on more dog than a Mexican general.
- Struttin' like a turkey gobbler at layin' time.
- He looked like a mail-order catalog on foot.
- He was wearin' one of them coats with flaps down the back like a damned scissor-tail bird.
- He shore was top-hand when it came to puttin' on the dog.
- Always went in for a lot of fancy riggin'.
- With their boots fresh-greased an' their spurs shined, they would hit for town.
- He came to town wearin' so much leather it was sweatin' him down like a tallow candle.
- He was wearin' a biled shirt an' smellin' of bear grease an' lavender soap.
- He had on more leather an' iron than the nigh-wheeler of a jerk-line string.
- All duded up like a bob-wire drummer.

Drinking

- Had his boot heel on the brass rail 'til it near took root.
- Wore hisself out a bendin' his elbow to look up the neck of a bottle.
- He liked to look at the moon through the neck of a bottle.
- Givin' some folks likker's like a tryin' to play a harp with a hammer.
- Extract of bob-wire was his favorite drink.
- He was mostly a yawnin' on the glass to give it a good polish.
- Nothin' to do except wear his boot soles out on a brass rail.
- He kept the bartender busy as a beaver building a new dam.
- He had an educated thirst that called for bottles with pretty labels on 'em.
- Nope, no water for me, I don't want to put the fire out.
- "Why I'm as sober as a muley cow," he says.
- Always exercising his arm to hist a bottle.
- It kept him busy a paintin' his tonsils.
- He kept going to town to see the elephant dance.
- He was lappin' up likker like a fired cowhand.

- His bar served a free snake with every drink.
- That's the biggest snake I ever saw without the aid of likker.
- He suffered with a disease called bottle fever.
- Thet likker done et its way plumb to my boot heels.
- It don't take no backbone to belly up to a bar.
- A corkscrew never pulled a man out of a hole.
- Yuh might be the best bar-dog as ever waved a bar-rag, but I don't crave yuh a spittin' tobacco juice in the bottle to give it a good color.

Drunk

- He was more drunk than a peach-orchard sow.
- So drunk he couldn't hit the ground with his hat in three tries.
- He ended up with a brindle taste in his mouth.
- The way he spraddled down the street yu'd think walkin' was a lost art.
- He was drunkern' a fiddler's clerk.
- So shaky he couldn't pour whiskey into a barrel with the end knocked out.
- He drank so much hair-oil he had to eat moth-balls to keep down the fur.
- Drank till his boots wouldn't track an' his feet were a burden.
- So drunk he started seein' things that ain't there.
- Had a headache so big it wouldn't fit into a hoss corral.
- Woke up with his head feelin' big 'nough to eat hay with the hosses.
- He started givin' the town hell with the hide off.
- He bowlegged it over to the bar to inoculate hisself agin' snake bites.
- He was usually lit up like a honky-tonk on a Saturday night.
- He was shore havin' hisself a high-heeled time.
- They came a pilin' out of that saloon like red ants out of a burnin' log.
- He was as drunk as a hillbilly at a rooster fight.
- Mostly drunkern' a biled owl.
- His crop was freighted with scamper juice.
- Full of piss an' vinegar, he turns his wolf loose.

- He had a full-growed case of booze blind.
- He never knowed he had a twin brother 'til he looked in the mirror behind the bar.
- His breath was near strong 'nough to crack a mirror.

Dry
- He forgot what water looks like lessen' it's in a pail or a trough.
- Things was drier'n jerked buffalo in an empty water barrel.
- The river-bed was as dry as a tobacco box.
- As dry as a covered bridge.
- Driern' a cork leg.
- Not rain 'nough to wet the whistle of a screech-owl.
- Dry as the dust in a mummy's pocket.
- As thirsty as a mudhen on a tin roof.
- Driern' an empty water barrel.
- So dry he had to prime hisself to spit.

Dude, or Drugstore Cowboy
- One of them stall-fed tenderfeet.
- He's never been closer to a cow than a milk wagon.
- Closest he's been to a cow is a T-bone steak.
- He's shore pea-green if I ever saw one.
- Ridin' a drugstore stool was his idea of being a cowboy.

Dumb
- He couldn't track a fat squaw through a snowdrift.
- Had no more sense than a little duffer with a big navel.
- So dumb he couldn't teach a hen to cluck.
- He's as shy of brains as a terrapin is of feathers.
- Don't know which end a cow quits the ground first.
- His brains don't weigh an ounce of ideas to the ton.
- He couldn't cut a lame cow from the shade of a tree.
- All he knows about brains is yuh can buy 'em scrambled.
- He couldn't even drive a nail in a snowbank.
- I'd as soon teach a bull calf to drink as argue with him.
- He couldn't hit a bull's ass with a banjo.
- About as harmless as an old lady chambermaid.

He ain't got sense 'nough to spit downwind.

- His brain capacity wouldn't make a drinkin' cup for a hummin' bird.
- Why, he'd orter be playin' with a string of spools.
- There's nothin' dumber than a sheep except the man as herds them.
- He don't know no more than a hog does of a ruffled shirt.
- He ain't got sense 'nough to spit downwind.
- His brain cavity is shore pretty small.
- He couldn't head a hobbled goose in a narrow lane.
- Knows less than a hog does about a hip pocket in a bathin' suit.
- He don't even know sic 'em.
- His head is so hollow he has to talk with his hands to keep away from the echo.
- He couldn't flag down a gut wagon.
- Hasn't got the brains of a grasshopper.
- He musta' been in the basement when they handed out brains.
- He don't even know the Injun side of a hoss.
- Couldn't track an elephant in ten feet of snow.
- He never got past the flyleaf of a first-grade primer.
- Can't tell skunks from housecats.
- When I make an all-fired jackass outen' myself I don't crave no witnesses.
- Got nothin' under his hat but hair.
- Don't know 'nough to pack guts to a bear.
- His thinker is plumb puny.
- He couldn't find a football in a washtub.
- Couldn't follow a load of loose hay across a forty-acre field of fresh snow.
- He couldn't track a wagon through a mud puddle.
- As chuckleheaded as a prairie dog.
- Don't know dung from wild honey.
- He could be plenty ignorant without strugglin' to make a job out of it.
- He couldn't find a bell-cow in his own bed.
- Had no more tact than a bull going through a fence.
- He'd walk into a river so's he could drink standin' up.

- He couldn't find his own butt in a back-house.
- Take 'er back to the startin' line an' run 'er thru again', slow.

Easy
- Like a kitten hoppin' over a caterpillar.
- Easy as throwin' a two-day calf.
- Like lickin' butter off a knife.
- As free and easy as suicide.
- More simple than a first-grade primer.
- Easy as a hoss-fly ridin' in a mule's ear.

Eating
- He supped his tea like it was hot solder.
- Hungrier than a woodpecker with a headache.
- Sat there paddin' out his belly with my beef.
- Usin' a coffee-pot big as a dippin' vat.
- Hungry 'nough to eat a saddle blanket.
- He likes one of them eateries with thick tablecloths an thin soup.

Empty
- Empty as a gutted steer.
- Empty as a burned-out lantern.

Failure
- He's caught in his own loop.
- His saddle is slipping.

Family Man
- Has 'nough offspring to start a school.
- From the number of his offspring he musta' been right busy.
- He shore kept the stork a flyin' 'til the sawbones made a plain track to his shack.
- He had so many kids he had to buy a wagon.
- His kids were as plentiful as ticks in a wet spring.

Fast
- Fastern' chain lightnin' with a link snapped.
- He was going like a bat out of hell.
- He took off like a cut cat.

- As quick as a lobo crawling a colt.
- Goin' like a cat with his tail afire.
- Fast as a Deacon takin' up a collection.
- He shore 'nough flee-hopped for the fence rail.
- He was plenty nimble-footed.
- Lightnin' hangs fire by comparison.
- Wouldn't last as long as a grasshopper in a chicken yard.
- Headed for town like a coyote for a campground.
- As lively as a lobo with a knot in his tail.

Fat

- He was fat in the middle an' pore at each end.
- Beef plumb to the hocks.
- With another twenty pounds she could a joined a sideshow.
- Most of his weight's on the spur end.
- Not overweight—just a foot too short.

Fighting

- He jumped him like a roadrunner on a rattler.
- I squirted 'nough lead into him to make it a payin' job to melt him down.
- I'll knock yore ears down so's they'll do yuh for wings.
- Laid him out cold as a meat-hook.
- He lost 'nough hide to half-sole an elephant.
- I'll kick yuh so far it will take a blood-hound six weeks just to find yore smell.
- Got hit so hard he couldn't answer Saint Pete's questions.
- Folded him up like an empty purse.
- Then there was hell to pave an' no hot pitch.
- I stripped him of the bric-a-brac he wore at his waist.
- I climbed up an' down his backbone like I was a climbin' a ladder.
- I still had 'nough strength to carve another scallop on my gun.
- He had too much spread, so I clipped his horns.
- Tied him in a knot an' hung him on a bob-wire fence.
- Just haul in yore neck or I'll tromp yore britches.

He was fat in the middle and poor on each end.

- I'll kick yore pants up 'round yore neck so tight they'll choke yuh to death.
- I'll kick yuh so hard yuh can buckle yore belt 'round yore neck.
- Looked like he'd crawled thru a bob-wire fence to fight a bobcat in a briar patch.
- So skinned up his Maw wouldn't know him from a fresh hide.
- It was mostly just a small-bore squabble.
- He cuffed his hat to a fightin' angle an crawled 'em.
- I'm a goin' tuh hobble yore ears pronto.
- I can't afford to get mad, cause my size won't let me whup nobody.
- If the Lord had intended us to fight like a dog, He'd a give us longer claws an' teeth.
- Mister, I think yuh just laid an aig.
- Knocked him ass over teakettle.

Frame of Mind

- He felt like a broomtail in a cornfield.
- He's so hen-pecked he moults twice a year.
- Was as worried as a duck in a desert.
- As uncomfortable as a camel in the Klondike.
- About as refreshing as bein' burned at the stake.

Friends

- They got along like two pups in a basket.
- Friends close 'nough to use the same toothpick.
- They got along like two shoats in a pigpen.
- Get along as peaceful as two six-guns on the same belt.
- No more trouble 'tween them than between a kitten an' a warm brick.
- He'd back yuh right up to hell's backdoor.
- Friends thickern' calf splatter.
- He'd back yuh 'til the hens get the toothache.
- He'll back yuh till Settin' Bull stands up.
- Friends as close as cloves on a Christmas ham.
- He'll stick with yuh 'til they're cuttin' ice in Death Valley.
- Thickern' feathers in a pillow.

- Hell will be a glacier before he'll quit yuh.
- They're as thick as seven men sleepin' on a cot.
- Like two bobcats in a sack.

Gambling

- A few wins an' he was a wallowin' in velvet.
- His luck got to runnin' kind of muddy.
- He just sat there puttin' his money into circulation.
- The game started some small, but shore gathered a heap of moss.
- Lost his money like he had a hole in his pocket as big as a stovepipe.
- His luck kind of raveled out an' cleaned him down to his spurs.
- His pockets seemed to spring a leak.
- He never got nothin' higher than a two-spot.
- When the game was over, he didn't have a tailfeather left.
- I wish I had all the change the bartenders forgot to give me back.
- Nothin' in his hands but some very young clubs.
- He showed me a handful of five all wearin' the same complexion.
- He could never find 'nough spots on his cards.
- Wasn't long afore I could count my coin without takin' it out of my pocket.
- He was shore packin' a heavy load of luck.

Greenhorn

- So green we had to tie one leg up to give 'em a haircut.
- As shy around women as a green bronc is of a new water trough.
- So green he didn't savvy cow unless it was dished up in a stew.

Grub

- Dished up soup made out of dirty socks.
- Meat so tough yuh had to sharpen yore knife to cut the gravy.
- Chili so hot it had to be kept on ice.
- Lived mostly on pigs vests with buttons on.
- Deceitful beans—those as talk behind yore back.

So skinned up his maw wouldn't know him from a fresh hide.

- Meat so ripe it didn't need cookin'.
- To make son-of-a-bitch stew, yuh throw in everything but the hide, horns an' holler.
- The coffee tasted like water scalded to death.
- This hunk of beef acts like it was sawed right off the butt of some old range bull.
- That wagon dished up the sorriest grub I ever et.
- Coffee made out of water thick enough to plow.
- He likes coffee that'll kick up in the middle an' pack double.
- Coffee so thick yuh had to use sandpaper to get the settlin's out of yore mouth.
- His coffee was thick 'nough to eat with a fork.
- Had a taste in my mouth like I'd had supper with a coyote.
- Coffee strong 'nough to haul a wagon.
- I'll have my aigs dirty on both sides.
- Keep my aigs bright-eyed.

Gunfighting

- He reached and fumbled, which was a fatal mistake.
- The man who wears his holsters tied down don't do much talkin' with his mouth.
- A bad time to have his gun stick.
- The whine of a bullet is a hint in any man's language.
- He was near enough to hell to smell smoke.
- Reached in the air so high he grabbed goose feathers.
- It's sometimes safer to pull yore freight than yore gun.
- Death put the runnin' iron on him, a brandin' him for the eternal range.
- He could draw quickern' yuh can spit an' hollar howdy.
- He was packin' 'nough hardware to give 'em kidney sores.
- He had no chance of dyin' in bed with a preacher hoverin' over him an' a doctor takin' his pulse.
- He always liked a shade-draw start.
- He was glad to wake up an' not hear harp music or smell smoke.
- They let him down easy with their hats off.
- His finger had the trigger itch.

- After our powder burnin' contest, my gun was emptiern' a banker's heart.
- There warn't many tears shed at a boothill buryin'.
- You'll never find him a settin' on his gun hand.
- If yuh can't get the job done in five shots, it's time to get the hell out of there.
- Before he could reach his gun, he was wingin' his way to St. Peter to take harp lessons.
- A slow draw is a quick way to join the angels.
- He lived a life that would make them scary dime-novels look like a new testament.
- Fingerin' a gun ain't motion, it's plumb suicide.
- Packed iron so long he felt naked when he took it off.
- He hadn't shot nobody for so long his trigger finger went to sleep.
- Hot words lead to cold slabs.
- Pulled his iron quicker'n hell could scorch a feather.
- He wiggled his trigger finger once too often.
- Had so much lead in him we melted him down for bullets.
- Drawin' fightin' wages an' huntin' somebody to smoke up.
- We started a powder-burning contest.
- He's now riding a cloud, learnin' harp music.
- Now taking off his spurs at the Pearly Gate.
- He wore his guns low and loose.
- Maybe yore a man-eater, but you'll find me a tough piece of gristle to chaw.
- He was the toughest man west of anyplace east.
- That hogleg hangin' at his side warn't no watch-charm.
- He came home roped on and his toes pointin' down.
- Passed the time of day an' shook hands with St. Pete.
- He got halo gratis an' took his place with the angels.
- He was raised with a gun in one hand and a milk bottle in the other.
- Dug out his blue-lightnin' an' unraveled some cartridges.
- He set his guns a-goin' an' burned some powder.

Packin' 'nough hardware to give him kidney sores.

Hair

- He was havin' the cook gather his wool crop.
- When he took off his hat, he looked like a full moon on the rise.
- For hair he was fixed like a sausage.
- Them Injuns tried to find out how I wave my hair.
- Injuns gave 'em a haircut with all the trimmin's.
- His head was as slick as a baby's bottom.
- Injuns couldn't raise nothin' but hell and hair.
- I didn't have no hankerin' to let them redskins undo my hairpins.
- An Injun shore wouldn't take no blue ribbon at barberin'.
- I didn't want my hair a hangin' from no Injun's belt.
- Havin' his hairpins undone that way was a shock to his idea of barber work.

Hanged

- He climbed the golden stair on a rope.
- His neck was so short they took him out an' stretched it.
- He died of throat trouble.
- They left him garglin' on a rope.
- Gave him a neck massage.
- They tried playin' cats-cradle with his neck.
- Left him lookin' through cottonwood leaves.
- Left him doin' a mid-air ballet from a cottonwood.
- They tied him to a tree but forgot an' tied him too high so his feet wouldn't reach the ground.
- They hung him up to dry.
- Mostly used him to trim a tree.
- Left him lookin' up a tree.
- A case of a stiff neck an' a short drop.
- Gave him a rare chance to study the sky.

Happy

- As expectant as a sparrow watchin' a worm hole.
- Grinnin' like a possum eatin' a yellow jacket.
- As chipper as a couple of jaybirds.

He must 'av died of throat trouble.

- Grinnin' like a jackass eatin' cactus.
- As happy as a flea in a doghouse.
- Happy as a little kid pullin' a dogs ear.
- So light-hearted he's liftin' his feet like a sandhill crane walkin' up a river bottom.
- As pleased as a little dog with two tails.
- Grinnin' like a skunk eatin' cabbage in the moonlight.
- As goggle-eyed as a bear with a new honeycomb.
- As pleased as a little heifer with a new fence post.
- He was steppin' as high as a blind dog in tall grass.
- Purrin' like a blind cat in a creamery.
- His spirits rose like a corncob in a cistern.
- Like a dead hoss, he ain't kickin'.
- Grinnin' like a weasel peekin' in a henhouse door.

Hard To Do

- Like tryin' to tie down a bobcat with a piece of string.
- He might as well a been barkin' at a knothole.
- Like tryin' to scratch yore ear with yore elbow.
- As easy as trimmin' the whiskers off of the man in the moon.
- Like tryin' to find hair on a frog.
- Had about as much chance as a wax cat in hell.
- Like tryin' to find a hoss thief in heaven.
- No more chance than an Easter egg in an orphanage.
- About like arguin' with the shadow of death.
- As much chance as a jackrabbit at a coyote convention.
- No more effect than pourin' water on a drowned rat.
- Had about as much influence as a steer on a catch rope.

Hardtimes

- Times so hard the buffalo on a nickel started losin' flesh.
- Times were harder than a banker's heart.
- As worried as an Arizona bullfrog waitin' for a rain.
- Havin' about as much fun as a baby with the bellyache.
- His lip was hangin' as loose as a dewlap on a dogie's brisket.

Hardup

- He musta hard wintered by the looks of his outfit.
- Boots so frazzled he couldn't scratch a match without burnin' his feet.
- He don't own 'nough beef to hold a barbecue.
- If the saddle creaks, it's not paid for.
- He don't own 'nough clothes to pad a crutch.

Harmless

- Harmless as a pet rabbit.
- No more harmful than a newborn babe.
- Harmless as a bee in the butter.
- As harmless as a bull snake.

Hatred

- He's been packin' a grudge agin' me as far back as an Injun can remember.
- He was always lookin' for a hog to kick.
- I'm so agin' sheep, I wouldn't even ride through a flock with a wool shirt on.
- You'd make good buzzard bait if'n the buzzard could stomach yuh.

He-Man

- He maybe don't say nothin', but it ain't safe to ask him questions.
- Had a heart in his brisket as big as a saddle blanket.
- A man with fur on his brisket.
- Not strong on brains, but he ain't short on guts.
- He's a man that stood up before he was weaned.
- He was known far and wide as a he-bear with fur on his belly.
- He knew how to die standin' up.
- All heart above the waist an' all guts below.
- His craw was full of sand an' fightin' tallow.
- He stood out like a tall man at a funeral.
- There ain't much paw an' beller to a cowboy.

He must a hard-wintered by the looks of his outfit.

Helpless

- As helpless as a cow in quicksand.
- I had him trussed up as neat as a sucklin' pig for a roaster.
- He was as helpless as a froze bull snake.
- About as helpless as a worm in a bed of ants.

Homely

- A Montgomery-Ward woman sent West on approval she was.
- There wasn't 'nough room betwixt his eyebrows an' his hair to itch.
- His front teeth stuck out so far he could eat popcorn out of a jug.
- Face as long as a dried possum hide.
- He could eat oats out of a churn.
- Homely as a boil on a pug nose.
- His sour look would pucker a hog's butt.
- So sour she looked like she couldn't get the acid out of her system.
- Had wrinkles as big as creases in a boiled shirt.
- She wasn't 'zactly no parlor ornament to look at.
- Looked like the ugliest mare ever foaled.
- Had no more hair than a scalped settler.
- The bigger the mouth the better it looks shut.
- So homely even a hoss-fly wouldn't look at her twice.
- Had a nose yuh could store a small dog in.
- A jaw as long an' muscle-lumpy as a jack-mule's.
- Had a face so ugly it belonged in a hackamore.
- She was uglier'n a Mexican sheep.
- About as handsome as a sack of horse-shoes.
- Her face looked like the east end of a westbound jackass.

Horses (bucking)

- Hoss acted like he was a tryin' to chin the moon.
- Thet hoss hid his head an' kicked the lid off.
- That roan could buck off a man's whiskers.
- Hoss was a showin' his belly like he was proud of it.

- Arched his back like a mule in a hailstorm.
- The hoss just sinks his haid an' unloads him.
- He pitched as stiff-legged as a mad ostrich.
- That hoss couldn't throw off a wet blanket.

Horses (cutting)

- He can turn on a biscuit an' never break the crust.
- Says his hoss can turn through the eye of a needle.
- He can turn on a button an' never scratch it.
- That bay of mine can cut a gopher from his hole.
- He could cut fly-specks from a can of pepper.
- Can turn on a quarter an' leave 'nough change to buy a can of beer.
- My hoss will stick to a calf like a burr on a sheep's tail.

Horses (usin')

- So genteel yuh could stake him on a hairpin.
- Thet old hoss is dead, but he just won't lay down.
- Rode him 'til he was covered with lather like a barber had prepared him for a shave.
- He fogs up to the snortin' pole an' spikes his hoss's tail.
- His hoss was leadin' the race like an antelope would a hog.
- He was throwin' dirt in the eyes of a jackrabbit.
- Was a foggin' down the road like he's going to a dance.
- He punched the breeze an' traveled faster'n bad news at a church social.
- He shore was a skippin' through the dew.
- If he humps hisself much more, he'll shore set his belly a smokin'.
- He humped his tail at the shore-end an' made far apart tracks.
- He was a movin' faster'n a squirrel in a cage.
- He was goin' like the clatter-wheels of hell.
- Starts for hell-an-gone an' forty miles beyond.
- His shadow was always twenty minutes behind him.

Hospitality

- Slide off an' cool yore saddle.

- Get down cowboy, an' line yore flue with some thunder berries.
- Climb off yore hoss an' eat a bean with us, stranger.
- Hang yore hoss on the fence an' turn yore saddle out to graze.
- Fall off that hoss an' come on in an' feed yore tapeworm.
- Beans are a bilin'—ankle in an' put yore feet under the table.
- Howdy neighbor, lean yore hoss agin' a post an' come on in.

Hot

- Hot as election day in a hornet's nest.
- Hotter'n the hubs of hell.
- So hot it'd slip hair on a polar bear.
- Hot as the underside of a saddle blanket after a hard ride.
- The heat sweated me down like a tallow candle.
- So damn hot that if a man died an' went to hell, he'd feel like wirin' home for a couple blankets.
- Hot 'nough to scorch a cub bear's butt.
- So damn dry, the bushes follow the dogs around.
- Hot 'nough to sunburn a horned toad.
- We had to feed the chickens cracked ice to keep 'em from layin' hard-boiled aigs.
- Hotter'n a burnt boot.
- It was hotter than hell with the blower on.
- Hot enough to wither a fence post.
- The heat would loosen the bristles on a wild hog.
- So hot it makes hell feel like an icebox.
- So damned hot the prunes started a stewin' in their own juice.
- If somebody had stuck a fork in me, they'd a-found me well done.
- It took me two hours to blow a cup of coffee cool.
- So hot and dry a grass-widder wouldn't take root.
- Even the shade of a bob-wire fence didn't help none.

Hungry

- Stomach so shrunk up it wouldn't even chamber a liver pill.
- He dug in like a wolf after guts.
- His tapeworm was hollerin' for fodder.

- So hungry I could eat a folded tarp.
- I'm so hungry I could eat a sow an' nine pigs an' chase the boar a half-a-mile.
- He shore was narrow at the equator.
- I was so saturated with hog-fat that I sweated straight leaf lard.
- I et so much hog-belly I grunted in my sleep an' was afraid to feel if I had sprouted a curly tail.
- I'd shore like to grease my chin with a two-pound steak.
- He was hungrier'n a bitch wolf with fallen arches.
- I feel like a post hole as ain't been filled up.

Killing

- Pulled his picket pin.
- Shorted his stake rope.
- Drove him in the ground like a stake.
- Bored a hole in 'em big 'nough to drive a wagon through.
- I planted him shallow without a readin'.
- Shot him where he looked the biggest.
- Took all the slack out of his rope.
- Them sharp hoofs chopped him up real fine an' saved on funeral expenses.
- He landed in a shallow grave.
- He had no breakfast for ever.
- He won a pitchfork for the Great Beyond.
- Killed 'em deader'n a six-card poker hand.
- He fell all spraddled out an' too dead to skin.
- His hide was so full of holes it wouldn't hold hay.
- Left 'em as full of holes as a cabbage leaf after a hail storm.
- So full of holes he wouldn't even float in brine.
- Wasn't 'nough left of him to make a bullfighter's flag.
- They didn't leave 'nough of him to snore.
- Let sunshine through him like a pane of glass.
- Finally had his spurs removed at the Perly Gates.
- I sent 'em hoppin' over coals in hell.
- He was pushin' 90 before he finished his circle.
- It was a corpse 'an cartridge occasion.

- He had leaned agin' a bullet goin' past.
- The undertaker was ridin' high on a wave of prosperity.
- He packed lead like a grizzly.
- He was so full of lead he couldn't walk uphill.
- A bullet nailed him down.
- He augered hisself into a cold meat wagon.
- He became a free lunch for the coyotes.

Lazy

- Quit spittin' on the handle an' get to work.
- Nobody never drowned hisself in his own sweat.
- About as lively as a thirty-year-old stud he was.
- He was lazy 'nough to make a good fiddler.
- Lazy as a hound dog in the sun.
- So damned lazy even molasses wouldn't run down his leg.
- Mostly sat 'round on his one-spot.
- Always a settin' on his end-gate.
- Hardest work he ever done was take a long squint at the sun an' a quick squat in the shade.
- Was always settin' on the south side of his pants.
- As lazy as a chilled rattler.
- Even too lazy to smile.

Liar

- Could color up a story redder'n a Navajo blanket.
- Could tell yarns as long as a whore's dream.
- He was as shy of the truth as a goat is of feathers.
- Always be shore yore story is wider than it is tall.
- He was always airin' his lungs.
- He shore was a stretchin' the blanket a-plenty.
- He told mighty big lies for such a little feller.
- He always piled it on plenty scary.
- Lets his ears hang down an' listens.
- I might just as well a been talkin' with a pack mule.
- He was one of them medicine-tongues as knows it all.
- I got tired listenin' to his squaw talk.

About to get a hemp neck massage.

- He musta been on a campaign against the truth.

Liquor

- Why I kin get better likker by holdin' a bottle under a mare till she has to pee.
- Whatever jackass yuh got yore likker from shore musta' had kidney trouble.
- Likker strong 'nough to slip the bristles on a boar.
- This t'rantula juice'd draw blood-blisters on a rawhide boot.
- Likker strong 'nough to make a grasshopper fight a curly wolf.
- A drink as would take the frost out of a frosty mornin'.
- Strong 'nough to make a jackrabbit spit in a bobcat's eye.
- Strong 'nough to make a muley-cow grow horns.
- It's a wonder they can keep such stuff corked.
- A few snorts of thet liquid fire an' you'd be plumb numb an' unconscious.
- Likker as will make yuh see double an' feel single.
- Yuh couldn't gargle that brand of hooch without annexin' a few queer animals.

Lonely

- As lonely as a teatotler in a saloon.
- She was a fussin' over him like a sagehen over a wild goslin.

Mad

- He was ringy, riled, on the prod, on the peck, had his bristles up an' paints hisself for war.
- So mad he couldn't even bite hisself.
- As prody as a locoed steer.
- As cross as a snappin' turtle.
- Mad 'nough to kick his own dog.
- Fit to be boiled down for glue.
- A screechin' like a plucked jay-bird.
- Mad 'nough to eat the Devil with his horns on.
- So mad he could swallow a horned toad backwards.
- Loaded to the muzzle with rage.
- Sore as a frog on a hot skillet.
- Mad 'nough to kick a hog barefooted.

- Mad as a bear with two cubs an' a sore teat.
- Mad as a peeled rattler.
- He even dug up his tomahawk.
- He lets out a mad howl as would make a she-wolf jealous.
- I digs my boot-heels into his toes an' bears down like I'm ropin a bronc on foot.
- I knocked his jaw back so far he could scratch the back of his neck with his front teeth.
- Stomped out a growlin' to hisself.
- He stood there a filin' his teeth.
- Knocked the core out of his Adam's-apple an' he tasted apple juice 'til he got his cider mill a workin'.
- Mad 'nough to chomp a chunk out of his axe.
- He set about a sharpenin' his horns.
- As sullen as a sore-headed dog.
- Acted like he was raised on sour milk.
- Looked as miserable as a razor-backed hog a stroppin' hisself on a fence post.
- I busted his talk-box an' he had to go to the dentist to get his bridle teeth fixed.
- Madder'n a rained-on rooster.
- Humped his back like a hog goin' to war.
- In a sod-pawin', horn tossin' mood.
- He swoll up like a poisoned pup with mad.
- Shuts his face hard 'nough to bust his nutcrackers.
- A bellerin' like a newmade steer.

Mad Cow

- She crowded me to the fence then boosted me over.
- Thet cow may be a mother, but she shore ain't no lady.
- There wasn't any love-light in thet cow's eyes as she made for me.
- I fogs it acrost the corral like I'm a goin' to get my gal to dance, with thet cow a scratchin' the grease off'n my pants every jump.

Making Peace

- We sat down to powwow.

- He sent up a smoke signal.
- We all had a get-together.
- Smoked the peace pipe.

Mean

- So ornery a sheep dog couldn't get along with him.
- His family tree was a shrub an' he was Old Man Trouble's only son.
- As mean as gar soup thickened with tadpoles.
- Meaner'n a rattlesnake on a hot skillet.
- 'Bout as sociable as an ulcerated back tooth.
- Mean as a sidewinder in moltin' season.
- As sore as a bitch wolf in heat.
- As mean as a naggin' woman.
- Meaner'n a bitin' boar.
- Puffed up like a green bronc on a cold mornin'.
- As full of venom as a rattlesnake in August.
- Meaner'n a new-sheared sheep.
- A mean look that would make an icicle feel feverish.
- Mean 'nough to have a reserved seat in hell.

Messed Up

- As messed up as a grass rope on a cold wet morning.
- He messed up things worser'n a hen in a pile of cow dung.

Miscellaneous

- The Old Man up there's a stompin' out his campfire an' the sparks shore are a-flyin'. (lightning)
- Don't never interfere with nothin' what don't bother yuh none.
- No tree big 'nough for a short dog botherin' to lift his leg on.
- I reckon ye've smelt out the wrong hound's butt, old hoss.
- "Oh, is thet you, Ma" said the little porcupine as he backed into a cactus.
- I reckon the Lord done put tumbleweeds here to show which way the wind is blowin'.
- Most men are like a bob-wire fence, they have their good points.
- "Well, everyone to his own taste," the old woman said as she kissed the cow.

- He bled like a castrated elephant.
- He wore one of them round-skirted saddles as looks like an old hen with her tail feathers pulled out.

Money

- He's got 'nough money to burn a wet mule.
- Carries a roll as big as a wagon hub.
- Got 'nough money to be called Mister.
- Had 'nough money to singe an elephant.
- He was grass-bellied with spot cash.
- Had more money than he could keep dry.
- A roll big enough to choke a cow.

Nervous

- As jumpy as a bit-up old bull in fly time.
- Nervous as a prostitute in church.
- Scratchin' his feet like a centipede with the chilblains.
- Nervous as a dog dreamin' of catchin' a rabbit.
- Nervous as a long-tailed cat under a rocking chair.

Noisy

- As noisy as a calf corral.
- Makin' more noise than a breedin' jackass in a tin barn.
- Sounded like hell turned out for noon.
- Makin' more noise than hell emigratin' on cartwheels.
- He was bargin' 'round like a moose in a wigwam.
- Sounded like a herd of long yearlin's in a brandin' pen.
- So much noise it would give a boilermaker the jitters.
- As noisy as a hoss in a dance hall.
- Noise made a brass band sound like a rattle-box.
- As predictable as a belch after a big meal.
- Noisier'n a wind blowin' over an empty barrel bung.
- As noisy as a scrub bull in a briar patch.
- A voice that would drive a wolf to suicide.
- Noiser'n an empty wagon on a froze road.
- Made more noise than a hair-lipped hombre tryin' to whistle.
- Noisy as a fog horn in a funeral parlor.

- Worst noise since my old sow got her tit caught in the gate.

Noticeable

- As plain as red paint.
- Plain as the hump on a camel.
- He showed up like a tin roof in a fog.
- Prominent as a boil on a pug nose.
- As plain as an Injun's signboard.
- As noticeable as a new saloon in a church district.

Obstinate

- Obstinate as a cow with a sucking calf.
- Always wants to roll his own hoop.
- Always kickin' like a bay steer.
- Fighting the bit most of the time.
- Ornrier'n a rat-tailed hoss tied short in fly time.
- So obstinate he wouldn't move camp for a prairie fire.
- So damned ornery he wouldn't eat.
- He wouldn't give yuh standin' room in hell.
- As hard to pin down as smoke in a bottle.
- He's as long-headed as a mule.
- Only a fool argues with a skunk, a mule or a camp cook.

Old Timers

- Always a cowman from his boot-heels up.
- He don't travel like a colt no more.
- He's gettin' long in tooth.
- He lived when hell was frosty an' the jackrabbits still wore horns.
- He's been a gopherin' in these hills since Settin' Bull was a calf.
- So bowlegged he can't even change his socks.
- He's been ridin' since he shed his milk teeth.
- His cinch is gettin' frayed.
- Now got his saddle sacked for a long ride.
- He's nigh old 'nough to be my dad.
- His gun scars looked like a regular war map.
- Had a hoss under him so long his legs are warped.

Range so dry the bushes followed the dogs around.

- Been forkin' a bronc so long he straddles a chair instead of settin' like a human.
- So bowlegged he can't even set in an armchair.
- About a hundred, but like a yearlin' he ain't cut his eye-teeth yet.
- Like a steer he still tries.
- He might be plenty old but he ain't hung up his saddle yet.
- He was raised with a runnin' iron for a hoss stick.
- Just fryin' size but plumb salty.
- He's so bowlegged a yearlin' could run through his legs without bendin' a hair.
- He's as bowlegged as a finger ring.
- Been ridin' since he shed his folded three-cornered pants.
- He was at the age when he should've been forgettin' the she-stuff an' spend more time reflectin' on his wasted youth.

On the Dodge From the Law
- He just leaked out of the landscape.
- Took off like a scorpion had crawled down his neck.
- He shore was a churnin' up the dust.
- Fogged it out of the country like a turpentined cat.
- Heaved a prayer in the general direction of Heaven an' rode.
- Headed for the yucca country where the lizards are out all winter.
- Spent most of his time ridin' the coulees.
- He was always just two jumps ahead of the sheriff.
- He stirred up more dust than Noah's flood could settle in forty years.
- Makin' so much dust it don't settle all day.
- Had a hankerin' to sniff gulf-breezes an' rolled his tail South.
- His name didn't 'zactly tally with the Bible.
- He didn't get much chance to grow up with the country.
- He came a whippin' a mighty tired hoss out of Texas.
- Left home in such a hurry he forgot to take his right name with him.
- A man that looks over his shoulder at every piece of straight road ain't been livin' a straight life.

- Came a ridin' so fast his hoss was kickin' the rabbits out of the way.
- When he hits the breeze for a healthier climate he don't stop for no kissin'.
- Where he came from the brush was so thick the birds couldn't fly through it an' the snakes had to climb a tree to look out.
- He always packed one of them brings-em-close glasses.
- Him an' the sheriff swapped lead, then had a hoss race.
- Where his hoss is goin' he don't know, but it's a cinch he won't be late.
- He was always a thorn in the sheriff's short ribs.
- Had a posse campin' on his trail till he got saddle sores.
- He was travelin' far an' fast an' beddin' none.
- Every time he gets into trouble he tries to pull hisself out by gettin' down on his prayer-bones an' taffyn' the Lord up.
- He hit a shuck without waitin' to kiss the Mayor goodbye.
- He ran up the back stairs like a rat up a rafter.
- He came a ridin' out of the brush with 'nough wood hangin' to his saddlehorn to cook a side of yearlin' ribs.

Peaceful

- As peaceful as a church.
- As serene as a prayer meeting.
- Peaceful as a thumb in a baby's mouth.

Polite

- He was a bowin' an' bendin' like a pig over a nut.
- As polite as a preacher a talkin' to the devil.
- Polite as a tinhorn gambler on pay day.
- As genial as a bartender to a sheriff.

Poor

- The cattle looked like the runnin'-gear of a katydid.
- Steers were so thin we had to wrap them in cowhide to keep them from fallin' apart.
- About as fat as a well-fed needle.
- Steers so thin yuh could look right through them to read the brand on the off side.
- Cattle as gant as a gutted snowbird.

- Poorer than a leppy calf at a dry water hole.
- When I shook loose from the piggin' string of thet fever I'd shore lost a layer of lard off my ribs.
- As poor as a toothless coyote.
- As poor as a hind-tit calf.

Pretty

- As pretty as a fawn with a set of stag's antlers.
- As pretty as a little red heifer in a flowerbed.
- He's so purty I feel like takin' off my hat to him.
- The purtier the gal the worse coffee she makes.
- She was more ornamental than useful.
- Had eyes as shiny as seed pods.
- Dressed so he looked like a mail order catalog on foot.
- He loomed up like a tin roof on a sunny day.
- Eyes as soft as blackstrap poured on a tin plate.
- As purty as a little red wagon.
- Trim an' neat as a new buggy.
- As prim as a preacher's wife at a prayer meetin'.
- She was as sweet an' mild as barnyard milk.
- As handsome as an ace-full of queens.
- Pretty as a basket of chips.
- Handsome as a new stake-rope on a thirty-dollar pony.

Proud

- Started walkin' like a tomcat in thin mud.
- Was walkin' like a dog had pissed on his off leg.
- He was all swoll up like a carbuncle.
- As full of pride as a bull is of wind in corn time.
- Prouder'n a roadrunner with a fresh-caught rattler.
- He swelled up till he busted his surcingle.
- Struttin' like a turkey gobbler in a hen pen.

Puny

- He shore was paperbacked.
- His cough sounded like an overture at a funeral.
- Didn't have 'nough wind to let a healthy poop.

- Looked like he was made of butter.
- His lungs wasn't stronger'n a hummingbird's.
- As helpless as a froze snake.
- So puny he couldn't pull his hat off.
- So weak he couldn't lick his upper lip.
- A sick kitten was plumb robust beside him.
- He was as weak as a dragged cat.
- So weak he had to lean against a post to spit.
- Not 'nough wind to blow out a candle.
- As weak as a gutted coyote.
- About as puny as a tick-fevered dogie.

Quick

- Like the first rattle out of the box.
- Quicker'n an old maid can crawl under a bed.
- He crawled that jigger's hump quicker'n hell can scorch a feather.
- Quicker'n a flea hoppin' out of danger.
- His money didn't last as long as a rattler in a cowboy's boot.
- They all scattered like a bunch of snowbirds.
- They went a hoppin' away like a bunch of tree frogs.
- He quit the country quicker'n a keg of cider at barn raisin' time.
- He didn't last as long as a boiled shirt in a bear fight.

Quiet

- As quiet as a discarded feather duster.
- So quiet yuh could hear daylight coming.
- As quiet as the whisper of leaves on a calm day.
- Silent as a tree full of owls.
- As still as a stone cow.
- As quiet as a breast-fed baby.
- Quiet as a hossthief after a hangin'.
- As quiet as a thief in a hencoop.
- As placid as a duck pond.
- Quiet as a sick cow in a snowbank.
- As quiet as a stone wall.

Range Condition

- Grass belly deep on a tall camel.
- Range looked like Hell with all the folks moved out.
- There wasn't 'nough grass to chink 'tween the ribs of a sand flea.
- Brush so thick the rabbits had to climb a tree to look out.
- Range so dry it couldn't support a horned toad.
- Not 'nough grass to winter a prairie dog.
- Cattle so thin they looked like they only had one gut.
- Another month without rain an' we'll have a herd of jerky on the hoof.
- Not 'nough grass to wad a smooth-bore shotgun.
- Cows looked like the runnin' gear of a grasshopper.

Recognize

- I'd know him in hell with his hide burned off.
- He could eye-ball a man a mile away.
- I'd know his ashes in a whirlwind.

Religion

- A lot of folks would do more prayin' could they find a soft spot for their knees.
- Listenin' to psalms an' exhortations on sin wasn't his bowl of soup.
- Had no use for some double-dyed hypocrite a gettin' down on his prayer-bones an' taffyn' the Lord up.
- Most of his religion was in his wife's name.
- He was raised on prunes an' proverbs.

Restless

- I've been here so long the rust's beginnin' to flake off on me.
- Always ridin' 'round like a hornet in a bonnet.
- Mostly just wanderin' 'round like a pony with his bridle off.
- Movin' 'round like a hen on a hot griddle.
- I want to wear out a couple more saddles before I pick me out a corral.
- He'd rather leave his hide on a fence than stay in a corral.
- Always a fightin' the bit to get to some other place.

**Cattle so thin they had to be wrapped in cowhide
to keep 'em from fallin' apart.**

- He's like a loose hoss full of cockleburs.
- Had so much iron in his system he'd rust if he stayed in one place.

Rustling

- He quit rustlin' cows for the good of his gullet.
- When yuh see a man a grubbin' an' whittlin' on the ears of a calf yuh can bet he's a cow thief.
- His calves don't suck the right cows.
- Thieves an' killin' were so thick yu'd think they had a bill of sale on the whole damn country.
- He shore was handy with a runnin' iron.
- Looks like his cows have a calf every day.
- He ran a butchershop an' got his cattle mixed.
- Always a pinnin' crepe on a cow's calf.
- He maybe couldn't see whose calves he was ketchin', but he could shore see where to slap on the brand.
- He'd steal acorns from a blind sow an' then kick her for squealin'.
- He couldn't resist pickin' up a rope that had a hoss fastened to the other end.
- He admired other folk's hoss flesh too much.
- Wasn't none careful what he throwed his rope at.

Scarce

- As scarce as bird dung in a cuckoo clock.
- Empty as a church on a Saturday night.
- Scarce as hiccups at a prayer meetin'.
- As scarce as upper teeth in a cow.
- Scarce as hen's teeth.

Short

- She wasn't ankle high to a June bug.
- Looked like he'd been sawed off at the pockets.
- He couldn't brag without a box to stand on.
- As short as a tail-hold on a bear.
- He couldn't see over a sway-backed burro.
- Would have to borrow a ladder to kick a grasshopper on the ankle.

- Lower than a snake's belt buckle.
- Lower than a toad in a post hole.

Shy

- Felt as out of place as a cow on a front porch.
- As shy as a green bronc at a new water trough.
- As out of place as a pig in a pawnshop.
- As shy as an old maid skinnin' a skunk.

Sick

- Had to have his bridle teeth fixed by a jaw-cracker.
- He had one leg tied up.
- Had a headache built for a hoss.
- He had to ride in the bed wagon.
- He was too old to suck an' too young to die.
- Felt worse'n a calf with the slobbers.
- He stood by the fence airin' his paunch.
- Looked as melancholy as a hound dog a-settin' on the doorstep of a deserted cabin.
- He was sufferin' like a centipede with sciatic rheumatism.
- He walked on roots instead of feet, an' the earth nourished him.

Singing

- He was shore a singin' with his tail up.
- Couldn't carry a tune in a corked jug.
- His singin' would drive all the coyotes out of the country.
- His songs were mighty shy on melody, but a heap strong on noise.
- Had a voice like a gut-gored buffalo.
- His singin' would stop a freight train.
- Voice like a bullfrog singin' bass.
- A dry axle could outsing him.
- He sounded like a long-drawn squeak of a slow runnin' windmill a-cryin' for grease.
- His singin' made yuh forget all yore troubles.
- His voice didn't sound like no Christmas chimes.
- Singin' as would make yore flesh crawl.

- Sounded like an iron wagon tire on a froze road.
- Sounded like he was sufferin' with the death rattles.
- He could near sing the nap off the hymns.
- His songs were mighty soothin' to the longhorns.

Sinner

- Long been flounderin' in the mire of sin.
- St. Pete wouldn't accept him as a candidate for a pair of wings.
- He shore wasn't pickin' any grapes in the Lord's vineyard.
- I shore don't want to be left out to starve on a bare range.
- He wanted to be up there where there is no end of harps an' free music.

Slick

- Harder to hold than a greased eel.
- Slicker'n calf slobbers.
- As slick as snot on a door knob.
- Slick as a greased saddle rope.
- As slick as a schoolmarm's knee.
- Slicker'n clay hill after a rainstorm.

Slow

- His hoss runs like he was goin' uphill with his hobbles on.
- As slow as a cow in a bog-hole.
- Slow as a snail climbin' a greased log.
- Took him longer than a hair-lipped hombre callin' his dog.
- So slow that if he ever laid down by a river to get hisself a drink the weeds would grow over him.
- He moves 'round like he's got hobbles on.
- So damn slow he couldn't stop quick.
- Slower'n a snail on crutches.

Smart

- He was as sure as cockleburs on a coyote.
- Had more smoke than a wet wood fire.
- He even knows what a cow says to her calf.
- As cattle-wise as a calf's mother.
- Weasel smart he was, too.

- I allow ye're as right as warts on a hog's belly.
- Smart as a bunkhouse rat.
- Wise as a tree full of owls.
- He sets deep in his tree.
- Smarter'n a squaw crackin' cooties on a papoose's foretop.
- Smart as a cuttin' horse.
- Like a prairie dog knows his own hole.
- He don't use up all of his kindlin' gettin' his fire started.
- He's as smart as a greased snake.
- He shore has a lot of wrinkles on his horns.
- He don't leave 'nough tracks to trip an ant.
- He knows more about cattle than a rabbit does about runnin'.
- He's upholstered with more brains than a sheep dog.
- He's red-hot as a ruttin' elk.
- The greatest law-giver since Moses.
- He knows cows, front, back an' sidewise.
- He don't need advice any more'n a steer needs a saddle blanket.
- He lived in the desert so long he knows all the lizards by their front names.
- A pet fox is plumb foolish alongside him.
- He's a regular chaparral-fox for smart.
- As full of information as a mail order catalog.
- As cunning as a she-wolf with pups.

Smell

- Smelled worse than hell on house-cleaning day.
- Worse than a packing plant before pure food law.
- Smelled as strong as a sheepherder's socks.
- He smelt stronger than a wolf den.
- I couldn't even get close 'nough to borrow a chaw.
- He shore was considerable whiffy on the lee side.

Smoking

- He strolled outside with a bag of Bull Durham in one hand while he gophers thru his vest pocket for husks with the other.
- He jerked a leaf out of his prayer book, an' commenced

He shore was considerable whiffy on the lee side.

buildin' a new life of Bull Durham.

- He always left pipe tobacco-furnaces to the sheepherders.
- He was makin' more smoke than a wet wood fire.
- He was puffin' a pipe so strong it would derail a freight train.

Snakes

- Snakes so thick you'd have to parade 'round on stilts.
- Biggest snake I ever saw without the aid of likker.

Snoring

- Snoring fit to shake the ticks out of his blankets.
- He was snorin' like a choked bull.

Soft

- Soft as a goose-hair pillow.
- As soft as bear grease.

Squareshooter

- He's as straight up as a wagon tongue.
- He stands as up and down as a cow's tail.
- He'll do to ride the river with.
- His heart's as straight as a rifle barrel.
- As honest as a looking glass.
- As open-faced as a Waterbury watch.
- His word was as bindin' as a hangman's knot.

Surprised

- Looked like somebody had shown him four aces an' a joker in a big pot.
- As surprised as a slut dog with her first porcupine.
- As unexpected as a fifth ace in a poker deck.
- Unexpected as a rattler in a bed roll.
- As unexpected as gunplay in a Bible class.

Swearing

- His cussin' would burn the grass for yards around.
- Such ripe language wasn't learned at his mother's knee.
- Their cussin' sounded like a mule skinners' convention.
- He was tryin' to keep the lid on his can of cuss words.

- Called him names that wouldn't improve a Sunday School none.
- When it comes to cussin', he don't swallow his tongue none.
- Lets out a string of cuss words as would sizzle bacon.
- Knew how to cuss in paragraphs an' had a regular tune to it.
- He could make a bull-whacker's cussin' sound like a Methodist sermon.
- He horned him with every cuss word he could remember.
- He made the air cloudy with his cuss words.
- Usin' double-barreled syllables seasoned with cuss words.
- When he jerked off the bridle yuh could smell sulphur.
- Cuss words as would peel the hide off a gila monster.
- He shore knew how to air his lungs.
- Usin' words so hot they would a burnt his throat if it hadn't been made out of asbestos.
- Cuss words just rolled out in a string of blue smoke.
- His language would make a bullwhacker hide his head in shame.

Talking

- He ain't 'zactly tongue-tied when it comes to makin' chin music.
- She shore was in the lead when tongues were handed out.
- They ought to hire him to keep the windmill goin'.
- Kept it up 'til he got a busted talk-box.
- Hey, quit yore pantin' an' swear a little.
- He shore don't have to fish 'round for no decorated words to make his meanin' clear.
- Say mister, will yuh cut the deck a little deeper?
- As full of verbal lather as a shavin' mug.
- Uses his breath for breathin' instead of mixin' it with a little tongue oil.
- As full of wind as a hoss with the colic.
- Had more wind than a little bull goin' uphill.
- Started fishin' 'round for a cowboy pencil. (stick or weed)
- He could talk the hide off a cow.

- Could talk a cow out of her calf.
- Didn't have 'nough vocal power left to bend a smoke ring.
- Had a voice like a rusty gate hinge.
- Just tighten the latigo on that jaw of yourn.
- He could talk a pump into believing it's a windmill.
- The silence was as brittle as glass.
- He could argue a gopher into climbing a tree.
- Just keep yore gate shut for awhile, will yuh?
- He could talk so fast yuh could smell sulphur.
- Sounded like he was garglin' his throat with axle grease.
- He's such a talker he blowed in on his own wind.
- Mister, I think yore full of hoss manure.
- Voice so cold his jowls dripped ice water.
- Used language so polished yuh could skate on it.
- Put yore jaw in a sling, yore apt to step on it.
- His jaw was gettin' exercised a plenty puttin' in a big crop of words.
- Usin' big four-letter words as nobody could savvy without an encyclopedia an' two dictionaries.
- Save part of yore breath for breathin'.
- Usin' words that ran eight to the pound.
- Too much wipin' an' not 'nough paper.
- He bellered like a bull calf in a briar patch.
- His tongue would get plumb frolicsome.
- With no talkin', he was as helpless as a dummy with both hands cut off.
- A cowboy can talk better when he's a scratchin' in the dirt like a chicken in a dung heap.
- He had a voice like a burro with a bad cold.
- Had more lip than a muley cow.
- One of them flannel-mouth hombres.
- Always a coyotin' 'round the rim.
- Voice like a crow with a bad case of croup.
- Yuh wanta make that plainer?
- Talked like he had diarrhea of the jawbone.

Tall

- He carries his water high.
- So tall he has to wear short stirrups to save his boot soles.
- Built like a snake on stilts.
- Wears his pants pockets high off the ground.
- Built high above his corns.
- It would take a steeple-jack to look him in the eye.
- He was half again higher than a bull buffalo.
- So tall he couldn't tell when his feet were cold.
- He was as long as a grizzly's gut.
- Growed so fast his head pushed right up through his hair.
- He sprung up like a spring toadstool.
- He was as long as a wagon track.

Thin - Skinny

- If he'd a closed one eye he'd look like a needle.
- As lean as a desert grasshopper.
- He was plumb saddlesore an' gut-shrunk.
- So poor his shadow was developin' holes in it.
- Had to stand twice in the same place to cast a shadow.
- He was as slim as a bedslat.
- So thin yuh couldn't a hit him with a handful of gravel.
- So thin he has to lean agin' a post to cuss.
- Looks like he's just walkin' 'round to save funeral expenses.
- So thin yuh couldn't notch him in yore saddle gun.
- So thin it looked like we'd have to tail him up.
- So thin his hide flaps on his bones like a bedquilt on a ridge pole.
- Looked like he'd been weaned on a pickle.
- So thin he could take a bath in a shotgun barrel.
- He looked like a needle standin' up.
- So thin he couldn't cast a shadow.

Tightwad

- He was as close-fisted as beads on a string.
- He wouldn't loan yuh a nickle 'lessen yuh got the Lord an' all

Skinnier 'n a wet weasel.

his disciples to go on yore note.

- So tight he wouldn't pay a nickel to see an earthquake.
- So stingy he'd skin a flea for its hide an' tallow.
- He'd squeeze a dollar till the eagle started losin' flesh.
- So stingy, if he owned a lake he wouldn't give a duck a drink.
- If yuh shared a bed with him for six months yuh might feel yuh know 'em well 'nough to borrow a match.
- He wouldn't give yuh a sowbelly rind to grease yore flapjack griddle.
- One of them fellars as loans yuh his bumbershoot when the sun shines, an' wants it back pronto when it rains.
- So tight he'd get out of bed to turn over so's not to wear out the sheets.
- Doesn't chew tobacco 'cause he'd have to spit.
- He'd chase a sparrow to hell for the seeds in him an' spoil a good knife cuttin' him open.
- He comes to town with a dirty shirt an' a dollar bill an' don't change either while he is there.
- So stingy the Injuns don't go near his wagon.
- He lived in a house so small he couldn't cuss his cat without gettin' fur in his mouth.

Tired

- If yuh reach down an' find yore clothes cold, you've overslept.
- He was runnin' down faster's a two-dollar watch.
- As weary as a tomcat walkin' in mud.
- Tongue hangin' out a foot an' forty inches.
- Limp as a wornout fiddle string.
- Head a hangin' like a pantin' tongue.
- As limp as a neck-wrung rooster.
- Pantin' like a lizard on a hot rock.
- It now takes him all night to do what he used to do all night.
- Tired as a ruttin' bull-cat after an all-night prowl through the mud.

Tough Guy

- When he heaved a sigh yuh could feel the draft.
- So tough he had to sneak up on the dipper to get hisself a drink of water.

- He swoops down on purty gals like forty hen-hawks on a settin' quail.
- So tough he's growed horns.
- He always wanted to have fun before that old feller with the hay-hook comes along.
- He chews up nails an' spits out tacks.
- He an' his Maw were tougher'n a basket of snakes.
- As thorny as cactus.
- He was tougher'n the callouses on a barfly's elbow.
- Used talkin' words as cold as icicles.
- Had snake blood in him.
- He's as tough as a sow's snout.
- Eyes that would chill a side of beef.
- He's got more crust than an armadillo.
- A stare as cold as a banker's heart.
- As touchy as a teased snake.
- He was more dangerous than kickin' a loaded polecat.
- Grindin' his teeth like he could eat the sights off his six-gun.
- His favorite food was tenderfeet.
- He's a wolf an' ain't togged out in lambswool either.
- When he bellers scat, all the gals better run for cover.
- Yuh ain't so broad in the pants as yuh think yuh are, mister.
- You the stud-duck in this pond?
- So tough he planted radish seed with a shotgun.
- So tough he'd eat off the same plate with a rattler.
- When he goes a courtin', all the gals better curl up on their mother's lap.
- As cold-blooded as a rattler with a chill.
- Had the morals of a hydrophoby skunk.
- He was as hard as a whetstone.
- Lips as cold as the stare of a gila monster.
- It plumb made yore neck hairs stand up to look at him.
- Brace him an' yuh got a catamount by the tail.
- He had a man for breakfast every morning.

Tracking and Trailing

- Ridin' a trail that would make a mountain goat nervous.
- He could follow a woodtick on solid rock.
- Could track bees in a blizzard.
- He could track a bear through running water.
- Could hunt a whisper in a big wind.
- As easy to find as a fly in a currant pie for him.
- It was tougher'n tryin' to find hair on a frog.

Traveling

- Going 'round the coffee pot lookin' for the handle would about cover the extent of his travels.

Unhappy

- Looked as sad as a bloodhound's eye.
- Happy as a hog bein' dragged away from a feed trough.
- His luck was runnin' kind of muddy.
- He looked like a motherless calf.
- Looked like a throw-out from a footsore remuda.
- Looked as sad as a tick-fevered dogie.
- Looked so sad his ears flopped.
- Guess the smoke from yore campfire got in my eyes.
- Had more troubles than Job had boils.
- His lips hung down like a blacksmith's apron.
- Lips stickin' out like a buggy seat.
- Havin' as much fun as a baby with the bellyache.
- Lips hangin' as limp as a dewlap on a dogie's brisket.
- As unhappy as a scalded pup lookin' for a snowbank.
- As uncomfortable as a hoss-thief at a hangin' bee.
- He felt about as homeless as a used poker chip.
- Uncomfortable as ridin' night herd in the rain without a slicker.
- As unhappy as a woodpecker in a petrified forest.
- He was sheddin' tears as big as a fist.

Unwelcome

- As unwelcome as a tax collector.

- As welcome as a polecat at a picnic.
- About as polite as one bulldog to another.
- Folks go 'round him like he was a swamp.
- As popular as a wet dog at a parlor social.
- Unpopular as a bear in a hogpen.
- As welcome as a rattler in a prairie-dog town.

Useless

- As useless as settin' a milk bucket under a bull.
- As useless as tits on a boar pig.
- Useless as a knot in a stake rope.
- As useless as a wart on a pretty gal's bottom.
- Useless as salting the ocean.
- Useless as a dog barkin' at a knot hole.
- Useless as a .22 cartridge in a ten-gauge shotgun.
- As useless as a bob-wire fence full of knotholes.
- As useless as a four-card flush.
- Had about as much use for it as a bull needs tits.
- No more use than Noah had for tail lights on his ark.

Walking

- He terrapined his way back to camp.
- He shore lost considerable steam an' was a whistlin' like a wind-broke hoss.
- He was a-blowin' like a bull snake at a barkin' dog.

Washing

- He snorts in the wash-basin a few times to get the sleep out of his eyes.
- Paws over a towel that has been plumb popular from its complexion.

Water

- Water was hip deep on a tall Injun.
- Yuh might have to chaw it before yuh could swaller it, but if yore thirsty 'nough it's damn good drinkin'.
- Water deep 'nough to wash a high hoss's withers in.
- Thet gyp water was so mean it would run uphill an' wanted to stay in a jug.

**By all odds the finest blanket companion in the country
she was.**

Welcome

- As welcome as a pardon to a lifer.
- Welcome as an invitation to split a quart.
- Had more friends than there is fiddlers in hell.
- As welcome as Santa Claus in an orphan asylum.
- As welcome as a pat straight flush.

Wet

- So wet he carried a canoe on his pack hoss.
- The Lord shore musta' pulled the cork.
- Wet 'nough to bog a snipe.
- The whole country was so swampy it'd bog a butterfly.
- Wet 'nough to drown a duck with an umbrella tail.
- Had everybody a-wishin' they'd growed fins instead of feet.
- It got boggy 'nough to bog a buzzard's shadow.
- He got bogged down to the saddle skirts.
- He was hopin' it would rain hard 'nough so's he'd have to dive down to grease the windmill.

Wild

- Wilder'n a turpentined cat.
- As wild as a corn-crib rat.

Wild Cows

- That cow came out of the corral a stompin'.
- There's always some old stampeder a hangin' out on the edge of the herd lookin' for boogers.
- That old bossy cow walked through that fence like a fallin' tree through cobwebs.
- That cow wasn't like them harmless critters as wear bells an' are punched with a stool.
- Them cows shore ain't never been handled by no milkmaid.

Women

- There's only two things I'm afraid of, a decent woman an' bein' left afoot.
- Hosses an' wimmen will shore make a man go whistlin', provided he's still young 'nough to pucker.

- I don't like to have my haunches spurred by no drip-nose of a gal.
- She had about as much warmth as an icicle.
- She was a widow of the grass variety.
- He ordered hisself a wife from a matrimonial agency same as he ordered his under-riggin's.
- The photograph she sent didn't show up all the blemishes.
- The sky-pilot soon had them welded to the neckyoke.
- She soon had him walkin' the fence.
- Soon had 'em hogtied with matrimonial ropes.
- The only evidence of her husband's passin' was the black weeds she cultivated for a week or so.
- That little wisdom-bringer's so sweet the bee trees are gall beside her.
- She soon had him so civilized he'd tote a bumbershoot an wear galluses.
- She was so crabby she couldn't get the acid out of her system.
- Yuh can't turn a woman mor'n yuh can a runaway hog.
- Yuh couldn't a stopped her with a forty-foot rope an' a snubbin' post.
- As jealous as a hound bitch with her first batch of pups.
- She was as soft an' fluffy as a goose-hair pillow.
- Leave it to a female to put flavor in yore grub.
- I'd just as soon marry a orphan asylum.
- In spite of their fancy duds, most of the red-light gals had their hearts in the right place.
- She lived in the badlands where the lights are red an' the carpets soft.
- By all odds the finest blanket companion in the country she was.
- A grass widow is a dangerous critter for a bachelor cowboy.
- She wore so much paint she couldn't even blush.
- She had no trouble gettin' a rake to gather her crop.
- She was always willin' to surrender like a willow in the wind.
- She wasn't even fit for a drinkin' man to hole up with.
- A double-breasted female she was.

- She was as hot as a widowed coyote.
- She didn't wear much mor'n a sneeze an' a ring.
- She soon got used to runnin' with the drags of the she-herd.
- Gals came west to shake their loops at some lonely cowpoke.
- She'd strayed off the main trail before her soul was full-growed.
- Those fast city gals shore buggered up all of the home heifers.
- Their silks an' satins swished till they sounded like a high wind in tall grass.
- She might a had a short rope, but she shore threw a wide loop.

Working
- Sweatin' like a hog butcher in frost time.
- He wouldn't be caught on the blister end of no damn shovel.
- Well, don't strain yore milk a tryin'.
- He finally drowned in his own sweat.

Worthless
- He ain't worth a barrel of shucks.
- He ain't fit to shoot at when yuh want to unload yore gun.
- His family tree wasn't no more better than a shrub.
- As unreliable as a woman's watch.
- I wouldn't trust him as far as I can throw an elephant agin' a strong wind.
- Yuh wouldn't dare sleep 'longside of him with yore mouth open if yuh had gold teeth.
- His biography would have to be written on asbestos paper.
- A horsin' mare is plumb worthless.
- About as worthless as a pail of hot spit.

HORSETISTICS

Here's some figures I'll bet you never even knew about unless you like to dig around like I do for such stuff.

In the United States, where we live, there are between maybe 10,000,000 and 12,000,000 horses. Did you know that? Neither did I 'til I counted 'em. And them same nags are probably worth anywhere between $3,000,000,000 and $5,000,000,000. Try that on for size.

And to take care of them nags for a year for such stuff as feed, medicine, tack and riding gear, etc., would run up to maybe $1,000 or so for each. Such stuff alone would run up to a few billion dollars.

And, believe it or not, there's probably between seventy-five and a hundred million suckers, 'er I mean sportin' folks, that go to see the ponies run. My horsetistics show that while most folks lose their shirts, there ain't no figures as to how much they win, if any.

Did you notice that everything I put down is between this and that? Well I did that a purpose in case I'm stickin' my neck out. And I'll bet a dollar dog that in another few years or so, when this book is getting dog-eared, folks will say, "gee, things was shore cheap in them days, wasn't they?"

DICTIONARY OF HORSE TERMS, GEAR AND SUCH

ACTION: Horse in motion.

AIDS: The legs, hands, weight and voice, as used in controlling a horse.

ALTER: To castrate a horse, or geld him.

AMBLE: A slow, easy pace. The front and rear feet on a side move in unison.

APPOINTMENTS: The equipment and clothing used in riding.

BACK: To step a horse backward.

BANDY LEGS: A horse pigeon-toed on his hind feet with the points of his hocks turned outward.

BANGED TAIL: Hair of tail cut below the bony part of tail.

BARREN MARE: A mare that is not in foal.

BICYCLING: The act of scratching with first one foot, then the other.

BIGHT OF THE REINS: The part of the reins passing between thumb and fingers and out the top of the hand.

BITING THE DUST: Being thrown from a bronc.

BITTING RIG: A combination of bridle, harness pad and crupper. Used to teach horse to flex at the poll.

BLACK POINTS: Mane, tail and legs black or darker than rest of horse.

BLEMISH: Any mark or deformity that diminishes the beauty but does not affect usefulness.

BLOWING A STIRRUP: Losing a stirrup.

BOOGIN' 'EM IN: When rider fails to scratch horse.

BOSAL: That part of hackamore that fits over the nose.

BRAND: A mark of identification, usually burned in.

BRIDLE: Rein, bit and headstall compose a bridle.

BRONCO: Unbroken horse.

BROOM TAIL: A western range horse; a poor, ill-kept horse of uncertain breed.

BACK JUMPING: Antics of a bronc trying to throw rider.

BUCK-KNEED: Knees bent forward.

BUGEYED: Eye protruding; horse usually cannot see well.

BULLDOGGER: A steer wrestler.

CALF-KNEED: Opposite of buck-kneed; knees bent backward.

CANTER: A three-beat gait, a moderate, easy, collected gallop.

CANTLE: The back of a saddle.

CANNON: The lower leg bone below knee and below hock.

CASTRATION: Removal of testicles. A castrated male horse is a gelding.

CAVY: A band of horses.

CAYUSE: A general term used to describe a horse of nondescript breeding.

CENTER FIRE: A western saddle with cinch hung from center.

CHAPS, CHAPARAJOS: Seatless pants made of leather, sometimes fur covered, for protection from brush or cold. Also spelled chaparreras, chapareros.

CHESTNUTS: The horny growths on inside of horse's leg; also called night eyes.

CINCH, CINCHA: A wide usually cord girth used on western saddles.

COARSE: Lacking refinement; rough, harsh appearance.

COB: A stylish, high-actioned horse used for driving and riding.

COLD-BLOODED: A horse with ancestry from the draft breeds.

COLT: A male foal.

COMBINATION HORSE: One used for saddle and driving.

COMMUNITY LOOP: Extra large loop thrown by a roper.

CONFORMATION: Structure, form and symmetrical arrangement of parts of a horse.

CONGENITAL: An abnormal condition that an animal possesses at birth, such as hernia.

COON FOOTED: Long, sloping pasterns throwing fetlocks low.

CORONA: Saddle pad cut to fit shape of saddle; has a large colorful roll around edge.

COUPLING: Space between last rib and hip.

COW-HOCKED: Hocks close together, feet wide apart.

CREST: Upper, curved part of neck, peculiar to stallions.

CRIBBING: Biting or setting teeth against manger or some other object while sucking air.

CRIOLLO: A breed of South American horse; a small, sturdy horse used as a cow pony.

CROSS: A dark stripe across the shoulders.

CROSS REINS: Method of holding single reins where

reins overlap in hands across horse's neck.

CROUP: Part of the back just in front of base of tail.

CROW HOPS: Mild bucking motions.

DAM: The female parent of a horse.

DEFECT: Any mark or blemish that impairs usefulness; unsoundness.

DOCKED: Bones of the tail cut in shortening the tail.

DOG-FALL: Putting steer down with feet under him rather than flat on side with four feet stretched out.

DROPPED SOLE: Downward rotation of toe of coffin bone inside hoof due to chronic founder or laminitis.

EAT GRAVEL: Being throwed.

EQUINE: Pertaining to a horse.

ERGOT: A horny growth behind fetlock joint.

EWE-NECKED: Top profile of neck concave like a female sheep's neck.

FARRIER: A horse shoer.

FAR SIDE: The right side of a horse.

FAVOR: To favor; to limp slightly.

FENDERS: The wide pieces of leather along the stirrup leathers.

FERAL: A wild horse. Has escaped from domestication and become wild.

FIADORE: A special knot on hackamore, exerts pressure at rear of jaws.

FILLY: A female foal up to 3 years.

FIVE-GAITED: A saddle horse trained to perform in five gaits, namely the walk, trot, canter, slow gait and rack.

FLAME: A few white hairs in center of forehead.

FLAT-FOOT: When the angle of the foot is noticeably less than 45 degrees.

FLAT RACE: A race without jumps.

FLOATING: Filing of rough, irregular teeth to give a smoother grinding surface.

FOAL: Colt or filly under 1 year old.

FOREFOOTING: Roping an animal by the forefeet.

FOREHAND: The fore part of a horse; the forelegs, head and shoulders.

FORGING: Striking forefoot with toe of hindfoot.

FOUNDER: Inflammation of the feet causing lameness.

FOX TROT: A short-step gait, as when passing from walk to trot.

GAITS: The manner of going. The straight gaits are walk, trot, canter and gallop. Five-gaited horses walk, trot, canter, rack and do one of the slow gaits: running walk, fox trot or stepping pace.

GALLOP: A three-beat gait resembling the canter but faster, 12 miles per hour. The extended gallop may be a four-beat gait and is about 16 miles per hour.

GASKIN: The muscular part of the hind leg above the hock.

GELD: To geld; to cut or castrate a horse.

GELDING: A cut or castrated horse.

GESTATION PERIOD: The length of time for the development of the foal from time of breeding, usually about 11 months.

GET: The progeny of a stallion.

GIRTH: The measure of the circumference of a horse's body back of the withers. A leather, canvas or corded piece around body of horse to hold saddle on.

GLASS EYE: Blue or whitish eye.

GOOSE-RUMPED: Having narrow, drooping rump.

GO SHORT: To take short steps, indicative of lameness.

GRABBIN' THE APPLE: Pullin' leather.

GREEN HORSE: One with little training.

GROOM: To groom a horse is to clean and brush him. Groom also refers to person who does the grooming.

GYMKHANA: A program of games on horseback. NOT A RODEO.

HACK: A horse ridden to a hunt meet. A pleasure riding horse.

HACKAMORE: A bitless bridle of various designs used in breaking and training. (From Spanish word Jaquima)

HAND: A measure of height of horses; a hand's breadth equals 4 inches.

HAW: A third eyelid or membrane in front of eye which removes foreign bodies from the eye.

HAZER: Steer wrestler's assistant.

HEAD SHY: Applied to a horse that is sensitive about the head; jerks away when touched.

HEAD STALL: The leather bridle straps exclusive of bit and reins.

HERD BOUND: A horse who refuses to leave a group of other horses.

HIGH ROLLER: Horse that leaps high in air when bucking.

HOBBLE: Straps fastened to the front legs of a horse to prevent him from straying from camp.

HOGGED: Short-cut mane.

HOOF: The foot as a whole in horses. The curved covering of horn over the foot.

HONDA: A ring of rope, rawhide, or metal on a lasso through which the loop slides.

HORSE: Not a jackass, cow or pig!

HORSE LENGTH: Eight feet; distance between horses in a column.

HORSEMANSHIP: Art of riding the horse and of understanding his needs.

JACK: A male donkey or ass.

JAQUIMA: Spanish bridle; a hackamore.

JOCKEY: The leather flaps on the side of a saddle.

JUGHEAD: Foolish horse.

LAMINAE: The horny-grooved inside of the hoof.

LARIAT or LASSO: From Spanish la reata, meaning "the rope." A rope with running noose.

LEAD: The first stride in the canter.

LEAD STRAP: A strap or rope attached to the halter for leading.

LIGHT HORSE: Any horse used primarily for riding or driving; all breeds except draft breeds.

LOGGERING: Pulling leather.

MARE: A mature female horse.

MARTINGALE: A strap running from the girth between front legs to the bridle. The standing martingale is attached to the bit. The running martingale has rings through which the reins pass.

MAVERICK: An unbranded stray.

MECATE: A hackamore lead rope.

MELLOW HIDE: Soft, pliable and easy to handle.

MULE: A cross between a jack and a mare.

NEAR SIDE: The left side of horse.

NECK-REIN: Indicate direction of turn by rein pressure.

OFF SIDE: The right side.

OPEN BEHIND: Hocks far apart, feet close together.

OUTFIT: The equipment of rancher or horseman.

OUTLAW: A horse that cannot be broken.

PADDLING: Throwing front feet outward as they are picked up.

PATHOLOGICAL: A diseased condition.

PAUNCHY: Too much belly.

PEGGING: Steer wrestler sticks critter's horn into ground.

PONY: A horse under 14.2 hands.

POINTING: Standing with front leg extended more than normal—a sign of lameness.

POLL: The top of a horse's head just back of the ears.

PORT: The part of mouthpiece of a bit curving up over the tongue.

POSTING: The rising and descending of a rider with the rhythm of the trot.

POUNDING: Striking the ground hard in the stride.

PUDGY: Short and thickset.

PULL LEATHER: Holding to the saddle with hands while riding a bucking horse.

PULLED TAIL: Hairs of tail thinned by pulling.

RAY: A black line along the spine. Also called dorsal stripe.

REATA: Spanish for lasso.

REGISTRATION: Recording an animal from registered parents in the breed registry association.

REMUDA: A collection of saddle horses at a roundup from which are chosen those used for the day. A relay of mounts.

RIDGLING: A male horse that has retained one or both testicles in his body cavity.

ROACHED BACK: Thin, sharp, arched back.

ROACHED MANE: Mane cut off so part is left standing upright.

ROLLER: Wheel in mouthpiece of bit.

ROLLING: Side motion o f the forehand.

ROWELS: The toothed wheels on spurs.

RUBBERNECK: A horse with a very flexible neck, hard to rein.

RUNNING WALK: A four-beat gait faster than a walk, often over 6 miles per hour.

SACKING: To slap a horse with a sack, saddle blanket or tarpaulin as a part of gentling and training.

SCRATCHING: Keep spurring in a kicking motion.

SCREWING DOWN: Sinking spurs into cinch to ride him out.

SEEING DAYLIGHT: Can see daylight between rider and saddle.

SHANK: That portion of the cheek of the bit from the mouthpiece down.

SICKLE-HOCKED: With a curved, crooked hock.

SIDE-WHEELER: A pacer that rolls the body sidewise as he paces.

SINGLE-FOOT: A term formerly used to designate the rack.

SIRE: The male parent of a horse.

SLAB SIDED: Flat ribbed.

SNAFFLE-KEY BIT: A snaffle with small metal pieces dangling from center used in training colts to the bit.

SOUND: Free from any abnormal deviation in structure or function which interferes with the usefulness of the individual.

SPREAD: To stretch or pose.

STALLION: An unaltered male horse.

STARGAZER: A horse that holds his head too high and his nose out.

STRINGHALT: Excessive flexing of hind legs.

STUD: A stallion, or a place where stallions are kept for breeding.

STYLISH: Having a pleasing, graceful, alert general appearance.

SUNFISHER: A bucking horse that twists his body in the air.

SURCINGLE: A broad strap about the girth, to hold the blanket in place.

SYMMETRICAL: Proper balance or relationship of all parts.

TACK UP: To put on bridle and saddle.

TAPADERA: Stirrup cover.

TENDERFOOT: Yuh shore are if yuh have to look it up.

THREE-GAITED: A saddle horse trained to perform at the walk, trot and canter.

THRIFTY CONDITION: Healthy, active, vigorous.

TIGHT-LEGGING: When rider grips horse with legs and doesn't scratch.

TRAVERSE or SIDE STEP: Lateral movement without forward or backward movement.

TREE: The wooden or metal frame of a saddle.

TUCKED UP: Thin and cut up in the flank like a greyhound.

UNDERSHOT: Protruding under jaw.

VICE: An acquired habit that is annoying, or may interfere with the horse's usefulness, such as cribbing.

WALK-TROT HORSE: A three-gaited horse; walk, trot and canter.

WALLEYED: Iris of the eye of a light color.

WAR BRIDLE: An emergency bridle made of rope.

WEANLING: A weaned foal.

WRANGLING: Rounding up; saddling range horses.

YELD MARE: A mare that did not produce a foal during the current season.

PARTS OF A HORSE

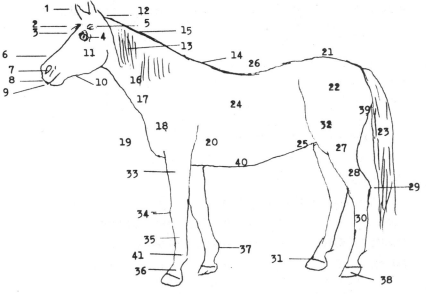

1	Ears	15	Crest	28	Stifle
2	Forelock	16	Throat	29	Hock
3	Forehead	17	Neck	30	Cannon
4	Eye	18	Shoulder	31	Coronet
5	Eyepits	19	Breast	32	Hip
6	Nose	20	Ribs	33	Foreleg
7	Nostril	21	Loins	34	Knee
8	Muzzle	22	Haunch	35	Shank
9	Lips	23	Tail	36	Pastern
10	Jaw	24	Girth	37	Fetlock
11	Cheek	25	Flank	38	Hoof
12	Poll	26	Back	39	Buttock
13	Mane	27	Thigh	40	Belly
14	Withers			41	Fetlock Joint

COLORS OF HORSES

ALBINO: Snow-white hair, pink skin and generally dark eyes.

AMERICAN CREAM: Pretty close to common cow's cream.

APPALOOSA: Snow-white hair over the loin and hips with dark round or egg-shaped spots.

BAY: Hard to explain but easy to see. Pretty much a mixture of red and yellow, the lighter the bay, the more yellow shows. A dark bay has more red. Bays always have black points.

BLACK: Generally have black eyes, hoofs and skin. Points always black. Tan or brown hairs on muzzle or flank not a full black, more like a seal brown.

BLOOD BAY: Near red, after a fashion.

BLUE: Light or dark shades.

BROWN: A brown horse is a brown horse. Some are called black because of being so dark. Take a close look at hairs around muzzle and lips. Mane and tail always dark.

BUCKSKIN: Like a red dun with some shade of yellow.

CALICO: Large patches of lively color—about like patched.

CHESTNUT: Very commonly called a sorrel. Coat is basically red. Mane and tail same shade as body. A pure chestnut runs from a fairly bright yellowish red to a mahogany.

CLAYBANK: Like a dun with shade of yellow.

COPPER: Take a look at a copper kettle.

COYOTE DUN: Kind of a grey dun with darker hairs mixed in.

CREAM: Any durn fool knows the color of cream.

DAPPLE GREY: Grey with some dappled spots.

DUN: A dun horse is very commonly called a buckskin, having some shade of yellow. It may run from a pale to a dirty canvas color with tail, skin and hoofs from near black to white. With a stripe down their backs they can look right purty. Some folks call them claybanks. Others call them gruellos.

FLEA-BITTEN: Grey or roan with some small black or blue specks or spots.

GOLDEN: Like gold—darker or lighter.

GREY: Most horses you think are white are greys. Kind of a tricky color, like an albino if it has light skin and hoofs and a white eye or two. Usually born blue or near black but by time is 8 or 10 years might be almost white. Color can run to dapple; steel grey or black spots would make him flea-bitten or silver grey.

GRUELLO: Grey blue like a mouse and always has black points.

INDIAN RED: Tan with a touch of red.

IRON GREY: Grey with a lot of black.

KATTY: Lack of uniformity of color. A dull dirty tone.

LEOPARD SPOT: With spots like a leopard or an appaloosa.

LINE BACK: A darker ribbon along back from mane to tail.

LIVER CHESTNUT: See at most meat counters.

MOUSE: Grey blue.

OVERO: Scattered patterns of color on dark backgrounds.

PALOMINO: A golden colored horse that can be real flashy with long silver mane and tail. But mane and tail usually run to near white.

PATCHED: About like calico.

PIEBALD: Black and white spots only.

PINTO: Other names are calico or paint. Pretty much white with large irregular patches in different colors. Don't be fooled with small color spots on a color or small black spots on rump like a chestnut. Pintos usually have quite a little white on upper legs and points.

RED SPECKLED: Grey or roan with bay or chestnut specks on predominantly white background.

ROAN: Hard to describe. The amount of white hairs mixed into the basic color is a good check. You might say a roan is most any color mixed with black or white hairs. Color might run from red, strawberry or sort of blue.

SCREWBALD: Any color except black and white.

SMOKEY: Blue tinge in the color—an obscure tinge.

SNOWFLAKE: Offspring of a blizzard.

SORREL: Bright yellowish red to a rich mahogany red.

SPOTTED: Spots of color on some solid color.

STRAWBERRY: Sort of red with white hairs or dots.

TOBINO: Large patterns of color on white background.

WHITE: A true white horse is white all its life. A pink skin and any odd colored hairs might point to a grey.

YELLOW DUN: A dun that runs to yellow.

ZEBRA DUN: Dark stripe on legs and withers.

VARIATIONS OF COLOR
ON HEAD AND POINTS, ETC.

BALD FACE: White over most of flat of face and toward cheek.

BLACK POINTS: Black mane, tail and feet.

BLANKET TYPE: Big patches of color usually on rear of horse.

BLAZE: A white area down face to lips.

CHINSPOT: A spot of color on chin.

CROSS: Dark line over withers.

EYES: Usually brown with black pupil and little if any white around edges. If eye is near clear with light shade between white and blue, he is called china-eyed, glass-eyed, cotton-eyed or blue-eyed. If frightened or the pupil has white around the rim he is orey-eyed. A horse with a mean eye is walleyed.

MEALY-MOUTHED: A horse whose color is faded out around the mouth, especially in bays and browns.

SNIP: Small patch of white over muzzle and often to lips.

STAR: Small area of white hairs on forehead.

STRIPE: Long narrow band of white from forehead down toward muzzle.

STAR AND STRIPE: Small patch of white on forehead and running down over muzzle.

STAR, STRIPE and SNIP: Small patch of white over muzzle and down to lips.

THE FIVE BASIC COLORS:

Bay	Black	Brown	Chestnut	White

THE FIVE MAJOR COLORS:

Dun	Grey	Palomino	Pinto	Roan

PARTS OF A HORSE SKELETON

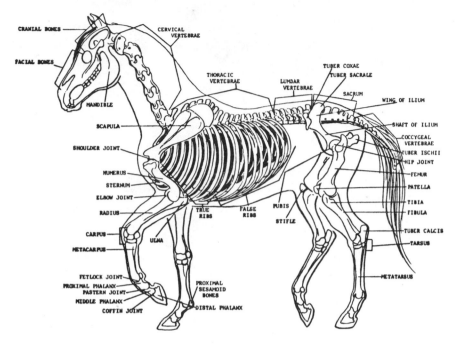

Skeleton of horse. (Drawing by Ethel Gadberry)

SLANG NAMES OF HORSES

Bangtail	Cayuse	Indian Digger
Boneyard	Circle Horse	Jughead
Bronco	Crowbait	Killer
Broomtail	Fantail	Knothead
Bucker	Gotch-ear	Man Killer
Buzzard Bait	Gut Twister	Nag
Calf Horse	Hammerhead	Plug
Carvin' Horse	Hay Burner	Ringtail
Choppin' Horse		Shavetail

CATTLE BRANDS

The word BRAND ain't nothin' special just to look at, but believe me it sure rates high in most of the civilized world and maybe further than that even. Of course there are lots of meanings of brands, but Mister Webster in his big book came close to hitting the mark where he says, "A brand is a mark made with a hot iron as on cattle to indicate ownership." The kind I aim to talk about are brands such as have been burned into the hides of millions of critters, including the hides of slaves, criminals and even them harem ladies we used to read about. But I won't even write about them critters cause I ain't never had no harem, so don't know too much about them. Do you?

When I dug back I found that brands have been kicking around for the better part of 4000 or maybe 5000 years. You don't believe it? But, it's a fact.

Hundreds of pictures and carvings have been found in caves and tombs showing old mossyhorn bulls with brands. Folks say these brands were probably used as much as 2000 years before Christ. I suspect that maybe Jesus himself might a run a few cows on shares or something while he was out spreading the gospel. Now remember that when I say 2000 years I mean BC, not BS.

I even read that those old rich kings and Pharaohs (now what in hell is a Pharaoh, anybody know?)—well, anyway, those rich fellers who could maybe afford a couple of harems each—used to brand their lady-girls on their forehead or most anyplace top or bottom so they wouldn't run away from them. Now I can easy see why them gals might a took up with kings and such, but why would any self-respectin' girl hob-knob around with a Pharaoh? Why you couldn't even tell were they man or beast. Hummmm, I wonder if some of them lady-girls that used to wear a piece of cloth hanging down over their face so they wouldn't be ashamed, might still be running around? Could be worth looking into!

And don't you suppose that I've even got a book that says that brands were being put on folks over in England as late as 1822! Why some of those fellers could near be alive today. They'd only have to be around 160 years old and I am over half that old myself. But even though brands have been in use for thousands of years they were first used in our country about 1522 or thereabouts. I guess cattle with brands on were first brought over from Spain about that time. Yet, cattle brands were not used to speak of 'til around 1775 and it was another 100 years before they really came into big use.

Charlie Goodnight and John Chisholm were among the first of the big cattle moguls to use "trail brands" on their big drives to northern ranges so as to know their own stock from other drives on the trails. Since that time there has been enough books wrote to make a pile of books from here to the moon. Some of them are true, but there are near thousands of books with enough blood and thunder in them to near float a battleship.

In the old days, folks had what they called family crests that they would brag about. However, brands have more or less crowded out the crests and stockman are now as proud of their brands as they are of their wives. Maybe even better, as a brand can earn a feller a living when most wives can't. Well, hardly! Should a rancher need a little loan to tide him over a rough spot, his brand was all it took to get him the loan. Course his wife would have made good security but bankers shied away should they have to foreclose on their security.

Now, a brand ain't just something you mark your cattle with. It identifies you, tells the world who you are, and a brand is often better known than its owner. I never did know who owned a lot of the famous old brands. Do you? And believe me, a rancher is proud of his brand. He'll take no sass from anybody and will fight at the drop of a hat to defend it.

Cattle rustling has always been a prime subject for book writers. It's a bad business to get caught at as the punishment for rustling is about like for murder and usually ends up under a tree without a reading or removal of hats. It's said that it makes a feller real mad to get strung up so's his feet don't quite reach the ground. Looks like a mid-air ballet folks say. And, of course, the doctor's diagnosis, if one happens to be around, was always the same "died of throat trouble."

Not too long ago, a feller came to my door where I lived in Montana and rang the doorbell. When I opened the door, he stuck out his mitt and says "are yuh one of the Potter boys of the old Diamond N down on the Cannonball?" I allowed that I was but it sure tugged at my old heart strings that he remembered our brand from seventy-five years back but had to ask me if I was a Potter.

I remember one time of Pa telling about when he shipped a couple-three hundred four-year-old whitefaces to Chicago. Before getting unloaded, he was some short of cash and went into the stockyard bank and said, "howdy, my name is Hank Potter. I'm unloading some cows down at the yards an' I'm a mite short of cash, can yuh help me out 'til I get squared around?"

"Sorry Mister Potter," says the banker, "I don't recall the name and I'm afraid I can't accommodate you."

"Shore, shore yuh know me," Pa says. "Diamond N from North Dakota?"

"Shure I know your Diamond N. Why in hell didn't you say so in the first place?" The brand got Pa his money which his name didn't.

So, now as I often set and cogitate, the old west flows strong in my veins. I like to think of the thin scattering of us old timers as well as the hundreds and even thousands of present day folks where somewhere deep down in their hearts is burning a teeny little spark of the Old West just waiting to come alive.

How many of you can recall your grandpa telling you how he got his start in the cattle business long before bob wire, railroads and such? Maybe 40 or 80 miles from a little cow town with mostly just a couple of saloons where you could wet your whistle with a snort of "tarentula juice guaranteed to draw blisters on a rawhide boot?" In fact, some of that liquid fire could make a man see double and feel single. Yup, give grandpappy the floor and somebody to listen to him and he'll spin a yarn a mile long, and with a shot or two under his belt just might confess to things he has kept bottled up these many a year.

Now, as long as I can't draw pictures pretty good, why I'll just write you down a little scenario as to how grandpappy might 'a got his start in the ranching business.

Picture a feller settin' on his hoss—a few dogies stand off lookin' him over—he sizes up the critters—takes himself a hard look up and down, sidewise, crosswise and slantwise—he slides down the side of his hoss—builds himself a little no-smoke fire out of a weed or two and a few cowchips—loosens his saddle girth 'nough to unfasten a little iron ring—puts the little iron ring in the fire—shakes out his twine—drops it over the neck of what he may later have to swear to high heaven was a maverick—

bunches together as many legs as he can grab—ties them together with a piggin' string, his neckerchief, belt or maybe a sleeve tore out of his Sunday shirt—with a diabolical grin slips a couple of green weeds through the now hot ring—does his art work for the day—rubs a handful of dirt over the hide picture he just made, so it will look kind of old—scuffs the little ring in the dirt to cool it—stomps out the little fire—replaces the little ring on the latigo strap—ties loose the one-time maverick—coils his twine and hangs it on the saddle.

Then he freezes though it's 110 in the shade, of which there ain't none—stares at a puff of dust in front of him—lifts his now bulging eyes as he hears what could have been the distant crash of thunder, which it wasn't—trips over his spurs as he jumps to tighten his saddle girth—climbs up the side of his hoss—clamps his laigs under his hoss's belly—buries his hooks in soft flesh, which means, get goin' hoss and muy pronto—changes his hoss's head from where it wants to go home to another direction where hoss tracks maybe don't show up so good—feels to see if his 30-30 is under his leg—his .45 rubbin' his thigh—pulls his hat down tight with thong under his chin—cranks his neck around to look backwards—keeps his eye out for badger holes—wonders if his hoss can outrun the jackrabbit ahead—prays to his Maker that his hoss can catch the rabbit who seems to be gaining on him. P.S. grandpa beat the bunny.

Well, sir, I will have to admit to me getting the diarrhea of the jawbone once in a while but I started to tell you about brands and such and I still aim to do it. I will have to admit that ranchers, cowboys and gals have made tracks a foot deep in our history. I know of a fellow who has written maybe a couple dozen stacks of books about them, and though I haven't lived on a ranch for enough years to make the tears start to follow a furrow down my old weatherbeat cheeks, I have even wrote a couple of books myself.

Well, it's easy to see that I am off on the wrong foot again. So, instead of me fixin' up a story about how to read brands and their makeup and use, I am going to let another fellow do it for me. I have added fifty or so brands of general interest but will let him tell the story.

So, thanks to Hobart E. Stocking and to *The Cattlemen Magazine,* official publication of Texas and Southwestern Cattle Raisers Association, 1301 West Seventh Street, Fort Worth, Texas, Tarrant County, zip 76100, United States of America.

Good thing you fellers have got a short name else I would've run out of paper.

CATTLE BRANDS

by Hobart E. Stocking

SO long as the range was wide and free, the man who claimed the grass needed a brand large enough to read as far as he could spot a steer. An ideal mark was the "Rail Under the Tail"—a simple brand that began on the port side, aft, and ran around the stern to the starboard hip. It could be read "going away", which was the most common view of Longhorns.

Back when there was no fence between Red River and the Rio Grande, cattle were restless critters and a yearling branded in Indian Territory might drift before a few winter's winds to end up as a four-year-old on the Gulf Coast. This was a nuisance but no stockman would admit it a total loss if the animal was well-marked. Every rancher had a few strays on his own grass and on the assumption that his neighbor would do the same, he pushed drifted stock homeward. Frequently he did not push them very hard nor very far but it was a nice gesture and one carried through more frequently than you might think.

Moreover, as a rancher tallied out Longhorns to a passing buyer he made note of stray brands among his stock and when the sale was completed he searched what newspapers there were for published brands of other stockmen. Sometimes a cowman three counties away received a check for steers he had never missed.

A brand was a sign of ownership and a rancher could think of no better place to write it than on a live cow. With a "gaucho iron"—a plain iron rod or, as a last resort, a saddle-ring heated in a cowchip fire—he began on the left shoulder and wrote aft until there was no more hair to burn. When a steer bore the rancher's full name there was no mistaking ownership, no matter how restless the animal might be. Moreover, "name-brands" had an additional advantage—they were just as easy to read in winter when cattle wore long hair as they were in short-hair time and they were impossible to burn-out in any season. To blot so large a brand was the physiological equivalent of skinning a

steer and while Longhorns were as tough as their owners, few could survive such an ordeal. A good many thousand moss-back steers grazed on western plains or slipped quiet as shadows through Gulf Coast thickets bearing **SIKS** or **YOUNG** or **IRA** burned the full length and breadth of one side. They belonged to M. L. Sikes or Andy Young or Ira Boone and every cowman within a radius of a couple of hundred miles knew it and generally let.well enough alone.

In 1874, J. F. Glidden of De Kalb, Illinois, patented barbed wire. Most stockmen would have nothing to do with the nefarious invention but the rancher who did throw up a fence, thereby shutting off drifting cattle, forced his neighbor to the north to build another fence in order to ward off a concentration of drifters on his range.

Not long after its introduction, "bobwire" had cut the open range into ten-section feed lots. By then Longhorn cows had been contaminated by tenderfooted Herefords and their shorter-horned offspring could not withstand the shock of a large brand. In addition, cow-hides had taken a turn for the better and could be sold for cash: a hide with a large burn brought less than one with a small brand. Ranchers bowed to the demand and while at all times they sought to enlarge their spread, they reduced the size of their brand.

As smaller marks on cowhide had wider use, stockmen developed a brand symbolism as logical as McGuffy's Reader but as complicated as Egyptian hieroglyphics to the uninitiated. Logically, brands read from left to right from top to bottom and, where necessary, from outside inward. But to complicate their literal translation, some brands were standing, others lazy; some were boxed and others plain crazy. There was one simple **HEL**—designed and chosen on the basis that the place it named was right famous, even in cow country, and that any rustler tampering with the mark would get just that.

Some brands dragged; others tumbled. A good many either flew, ran or walked. The latter might seem slow to the uninitiated but to ranchers a "slow" brand was simply one not registered with the local cattleman's association or at the nearest county courthouse.

Two simple marks upright on cowhide, thus: II , was the "Figure Leven" which was registered as the "Standing Eleven" to distinguish it from the same design in a horizontal position, ▬ where it took the name of either "Lazy Eleven" or "Panther Scratch". In Longhorn parlance, all letters and numbers lying on their side were lazy and there were hundreds, if not thousands, of "Lazy B" ⚏ , "Lazy D" △ and "Lazy 3" brands.

Any number or letter which appeared on cowhide upside-down or backward, or both, was "crazy" but in cow-country it was never safe for a traveling rustler to assume that the owner shared that quality with his brand. The man who ran the "Crazy 45" ⇂S owned a gun of the same caliber and knew how, and when, to use it. The few letters which appeared on the same right side up or upside down caused no confusion in a country where children knew brands before they knew the lower half of the alphabet. The mark U∩ was registered and read by everyone, young or old, as "U up and U down". Simple letter brands with flanges like ⩜ were readily recognized as "Walking" although it is certain that the owner of the "Walking A" never took to that form of exercise except in dire emergency.

Back in the halcyon days when the nearest cattle market lay months of slow trailing beyond the horizon, marketable stock ranged in age from three to ten years. Even the wildest steer could be strong-armed into the routine of the drive northward but steers born, or rather made, on the open range were never more uncooperative than at branding time. It may be that the first "Tumbling" brand came about through a slip of the iron or a kick of the steer. At any rate, letters or numbers inclined to one side or the other, as the "Tumbling T" ⅄ were logically so-called.

To a man who ran a ranch, nothing was more logical than a "running" brand, which was simply a letter stretched out so as to eliminate the sharp angles. Marks like the "Running W" ⩊⩊ or "Running N" ⩊ were popular for several reasons. One of their advantages was that they could be easily and clearly burned with a gaucho iron —so named because it was the only kind of iron the Argentine gaucho used—or even

with a saddle-ring heated in a cowchip fire and held by a couple green mesquite sticks crossed through it. Brands with sharp corners in them were more difficult and in fact were best imprinted on a reluctant steer with a "stamp iron". This latter device was merely the whole brand in iron hammered out to specifications by the nearest blacksmith.

Although a good many ranchers had them, it was generally conceded that it was well to avoid brands which involved narrow spaces between marks of the burn or which included sharp angles. Should such a stamp-iron slip just as it was applied, and open range cattle were never placid animals at any time, the hot iron would burn across the narrow gaps and the entire area of the brand would peel. Such blotched brands were subject to dispute, if not suspicion.

Probably only those ranchers who lost a stirrup on the second jump ever made a contribution to aerodynamics but a good many of them had brands that flew. The "Flying H" ꓧ is an example of that type and the wing bars might be separate from the letter or connected with it, depending on the custom of the country. There were quite a few connected letters and figures among brands, like ꟽ , which was read "M N Connected" so that it might be distinguished from the same mark with the letters separate. Illogically, a steer bearing Ρ belonged to the "Profit and Loss" outfit and one branded ◖◗ was a "Damned Hungry Dog" although it generally had a wide spread of horns.

Ranching, even after barbed wire cut the open range into pea-patches, was never a simple life. Whereas now-a-days a man will do almost anything but sweat for a living, a rancher never did anything but, except in winter when he froze Naturally every sweaty or half-frozen rancher liked to see his brand in as many places as it was legal and if he could afford a pair of tailor-made boots his brand was likely to be a part of the design on them. Footgear was plain black in those days; these modern polychrome mudguards are right out of technicolor. When a stockman bought a new saddle he had his brand stamped on the cantle or skirt. If the drive to Abilene or Dodge City had been profitable there was usually enough paint left from the house to splash his brand on the front gate—the only plank and post affair on the whole range.

Whatever the brand, it usually represented a strong feeling held by a simple character. "I X L" was the trademark on about the best pocket-knife extant in 1850 and in that year N. Locke, who knew he had some good goods too, registered the mark and began hanging I X L on cowhide. The 6 I brand commemorated the beginning of the bitter struggle between the States and 5 7 marked not only the first cow he owned but also the year in which J. A. Alberthal began ranching in Texas. Eighteen fifty-one was the year T. P. Hughes came to Texas and 5 I marked about everything he owned there for the rest of his life.

Down in Medina county, Texas, Joseph Welker, an immigrant from Germany, registered the "Block X" ⊠ He explained that in the old country a man who owned a block of land was mighty lucky Welker owned a considerable block of acres now and he stamped it on cowhide with an "X" inside to mark the location of his new home.

Long before they ever dreamed of competing in rodeos, there were cowgirls cut from the same honest pattern as cowmen. "J H L Connected" ⌐⌐ was recorded by Jane H. Long in 1838 and it is still used to mark descendants of her herd. Rosanna West was scarcely dry before she was in the cattle business. When she was just one hour old on January 14, 1840, her uncle roped and branded a heifer with WR. Rosanna's heirs still use the same old mark now more than one hundred and ten years old.

Not all brands were as simple as A B C selected by J. P. Noble and burned the whole length of his cows in the 1860's. Even in small-brand times ranchers preferred the personal touch and they evolved designs incorporating their initials such as ⓙⓒ the "Circle J H C" belonging to John Harrison Coker or the simple Ǝ of Bob Evans. Frequently vanity was flavored with a dash of whimsey — the "Seven B" ꓶ of G. C. Brightman was a census of the number of Brightman mouths he had to fill.

Faith in the results of hard work, hope that the future would bring returns, plus a heavy sprinkle of all-around good luck were the ingredients that made for success in ranching. No man on the range could afford to relax from either work or hope and no cowman in his right mind would ignore Lady Luck. Some of them were so superstitious that on the rare occasions when they heard a silken rustle they kept their eyes glued on their cows for fear a direct look would frighten Lady Luck away. Others glanced up at the sound and the schoolmarms promptly married them. But they didn't change their faith in luck.

The "Chain Seven", 7 7 7 was an outright appeal to chance and circumstance by W. C. Wright who calculated that if seven was a lucky number, three of a kind would beat one. The % brand was fervent hope of its owner for a reasonable increase of his herd. One of the neatest good-luck charms and certainly one with the most pleasant connotation was the $ brand run by T. E. Money.

Gambling as they did against the weather, the market and even with the primordial urge of opposite sexes among horned quadrupeds, ranchers were bound to have faith in odd numbers. And when it came to counting their steers, the higher the odd number, the greater faith. When it came to expressing their faith in odd numbers in brands they had to exercise restraint: there were only a limited number of square feet on one side of a cow and the fewer marks they burned on any cow's hide the better price that cow would bring. Generally they limited themselves to three. There was the "Three D" ∞ brand of D. D. Davis and among many triplications there were: ◇◇◇ , ♡♡♡ , and ⧉ This latter brand was an animated expression of hope by the owner that he would always be able to tuck his feet under that many every day.

That ranchers may have heard of hazards of chance other than those normally associated with stock raising is indicated by the "Ace of Spade" ♠ registered by G. A. Wynne in 1887; by the innumerable "Diamonds and a Half" ◈ brands scattered through cow country. But M. A. Heart had so much logic in his ♡ brand that it is even money that he never saw a card.

Brands passed from father to son with slight modification and sometimes in the second generation they landed upside down. T 2 was the brand of the second Alfred Thomas. "Ninety-one Bar", 9 I was James Elder's adaptation of his father's "Bar Sixteen". I 6 Among ranching families blood was always thicker than water, although in times of drouth there were a few hard-bitten cowmen who were reluctant to admit that it was as precious. The "Seven X" X , the "XL" X and the "L X" X marked cattle belonging to J. L. Bivins, Miles Bivins and Mary Bivins respectively

It was inevitable that with as many cows as there were, with as many bulls who never let a fence interfere with their courting and with as many restless steers as there were in the cow country that some of them were unbranded. All such animals were an anathema to every respectable rancher and they did every legal thing they could to reduce the number. Mavericks—and the term includes all unbranded young stock too old to be following a cow—had an honorable origin and it speaks well for the ranching business in general that there is even such a term.

Samuel Maverick's brand was the "Running M K" 𝓜𝓚 and his ranch in central Texas was a small one. Maverick himself lived in town and his hired hand spent a good part of his time literally sleeping on the job. The logical result was that a fair percent of Maverick's calves went unbranded but since his neighbors were honest folk, within reason, they kept irons off. In time there was a goodly number of unmarked old stock ranging the thickets and they too were regarded as Maverick's and, eventually, as mavericks.

Although in general ranchers were honest folk there were a few brands which were outstanding and distinctive because they, unlike their owners, did not tell the whole truth. The letters COW were burned on a considerable number of bulls and steers, as well as on vagrant mothers of heifers, and they all belonged to F. R. Lewis who registered the mark in 1867. The OX brand was impartially stamped on 15,000 head of stock ranging over 300,000 acres in the Texas Panhandle and it was a safe bet that there wasn't a yoke of oxen among them.

Among the symbolic identification marks borne by western cattle there is no cow brand better known east of the Mississippi than the one which belonged to Colonel B. H. Campbell. When Oklahoma was yet Indian Territory, Campbell branded BQ . Although the original owner of the mark is long since dead, he left a legacy which is perpetuated in indigestion and in the thousands of "Barbeques" which crowd every highway. He left another legacy too, a bit of folklore related to the creation of a brand for the largest of all ranches in the United States.

When the State of Texas had matured to the point where the dignity of its legislators demanded a capitol building, they found that they had more acres than dollars. Texas made a trade with C. B. and J. B. Farwell, two Chicago financiers. In exchange for three million acres spread in an irregular strip along the western border of the Texas Panhandle, the State got a brand-new red-granite Capitol, all ready to use, in Austin

The Farwell boys immediately found themselves land-poor and with the aid of "Barbeque" Campbell they bought into the cattle business. For a brand for the new ranch Campbell chose X I T . The mark is reputed to have been chosen to stand for "Ten in Texas" which indeed would have made sense even to Chicago financiers. But like the COW brand borne humbly by a considerable number of range bulls, the XIT brand stretched the facts by one county. Actually the X I T range extended some two hundred miles over only nine Texas counties.

There is no doubt that Campbell must have had in mind other, and more valid reasons. The brand was easy to read; moreover it was of simple lines and could be easily burned on cowhide with a straight running-iron. In addition it was sufficiently complicated so that it could not be altered to a wholly different mark by an enterprising rustler. Since the X I T was literally drawn with a simple, hot straight piece of iron rather than stamped on in one operation and since even yearlings would not cooperate with the artist, a considerable number of X I T stock were rather shakily marked with uneven letters.

Whatever a brand might be, it generally meant a lot more than just ownership. For all ranchers past or present, young and old, John and Kathryn Honeycutt spoke volumes in few words:

"I first saw the —⊙— brand near Gillette, Wyoming. The Keeline outfit of Council Bluffs ran it there. I resolved then to start that brand for a little red-headed girl and myself when I got back to Texas and clear away from the Keeline range.

"This brand means more to us than just something to distinguish our cattle. It is a symbol of partnership between a man and his wife who both love their cows and their country."

Ox Yoke Pin

Rising Sun

M slash H

J Muleshoe

Pick and Shovel

Seven

Backward E 2 Bar

Teepee –

Flying D

LU Bar –

Double Milliron

Boot –

Fleur-De-Lis –

Shrine Emblem

Flying X

Bug

Aladdin's Lamp

Double Oarlock

Seven Up

Seventy One

Dice Five

Turkey Track

Wineglass

Two Dots

Sled Runner

Scythe

Keystone

HT

Mission Range

Rocking Chair

Broken arrow

100 CATTLE

Around Patagonia

EAR CROPS

OVER BITE

UNDER BITE

SPLIT

HACK

OVER SLOPE

HORN BRAND

UNDER SLOPE

OVER HACK

UNDER HACK

7 OVER BITE

7 UNDER BITE

CROP

STEEPLE FORK

SHARP

OVER SPLIT

UNDER SPLIT

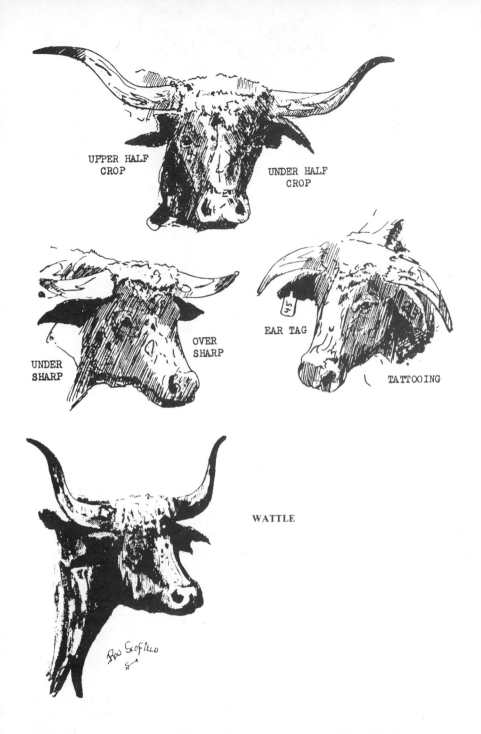

UPPER HALF CROP

UNDER HALF CROP

UNDER SHARP

OVER SHARP

EAR TAG

TATTOOING

WATTLE

RON SCOFIELD

Being that I was raised on a cattle ranch, I figure that a rodeo gives a man more for his money than any of the other games or sports. I even like rodeos better than horse-racin' which tops them all with something like seventy million folks going to see the ponies race each year.

The word "rodeo" comes from the Spanish and means about the same as a roundup, or a stampede, buckin' contest, frontier days, western days, etc. Back about to the year 1883, Pecos, Texas held the first rodeo where prizes were given to the riders. That's going back 100 years or so. It was probably just a bunch of cowboys got together to see who were the best riders and ropers. You didn't have to pay anything to watch the fun and folks just sat in their wagons and buggies or maybe straddled the rail fence.

That was about the time when a big man by the name of Bill Pickett was working for the 101 spread. Bill was a top hand and he figured to show the crowd how to 'rassle a bull. After Bill threw the bull to the ground, he set his teeth in the bull's lips and held him down without putting a hand on him. I guess that's where the name bulldoggin' got its start. Now I claim that Bill was "a feller with hair on his chest."

Rodeos, with their Western influence, have rapidly spread throughout the United States as well as in Canada and Mexico and are gaining a foothold in other countries. Boots, Western shirts, Levi's and ten-gallon hats are the coming style. Folks not only want to dress Western, they also want to use a lot of Western talk. So, I aim to tell you something about what you will see when you go to a first-class rodeo.

When you go to a rodeo you will have more excitement to the square inch than you can hardly stand. You set on the very edge of your seat and, when your heart misses a few beats, you grip the arm of your partner, if you got one, or maybe the leg of the pretty gal settin' alongside of you. Course, you will probably get an elbow in yore short-ribs for being so fresh. But, try it sometimes, cause you can usually talk your way out of it, or maybe even line up yourself a date—if you don't try to hurry things along too fast.

I remember one time . . . oh what's the use, that was a long time ago when I was a little younger.

Let's see now, where was I? Oh yes. Well, everytime a chute-gate is opened you can expect a cyclone or a tornado, or at least some kind of a critter to come out a squeelin' and a bellerin' with fire in his eye and a snortin' fire and brimstone at every jump. The feller settin' on top? He may look "as calm as a skunk in the moonlight," but his old ticker is probably thumpin' along at least three or four hundred per. I know from experience mine used to hit 500 without even tryin'. Of course the mere fact that the feller has to keep one hand in the air doesn't help too much, particularly when at times he would give a leg to reach down and grab the nubbin'. And worst of all, nowadays there ain't even no nubbin' to grab.

But, whatever happens, you don't see no handshakin' or kissin' each other by the cowboys. He don't want to be nurse-maided by having somebody even pick up his hat, or maybe help him stagger to his feet and maybe high-tail it to the nearest fence. Oh, if he had a broke leg or arm, why sure, somebody might come out and wrap a bandana or piggin' string around it so he could be ready for his next go-around.

Why, I've even seen them help load a feller into an ambulance if he got hurt real bad. Course, if the feller got full killed, they would probably write to his wife and ask where she would like to have his saddle shipped to, and probably tell her that he wouldn't be home anymore.

So far I have only talked a little about bronc riding. But that's just a start of the fun. How about all those other doings like bull doggin', calf roping, barrel racing, team roping, sack races, bull riding, wagon races, steer tying, wild cow milking, hide races, horse racing, to say nothing of the clowns acting up.

Now let's watch a cowboy ride a big overgrown 2,000 pounds of blood and guts that goes by the lady-like name of Brahma. Why, them big fellers with a hump on their neck have got snake blood in 'em and they are about "as sociable as an ulcerated back tooth." They'll hide all day behind a fence post just waitin' for something to come along they can disembowel or at least toss into the next county. One time I was settin' on a ten-foot-high fence takin' pictures, and one of them big fellers wanted out and took a dive at me. His aim wan't pretty good so all he did was to unpart my hair. But, he cleared the fence, and so did I, with m y camera on top of me as I hit the ground. When I looked up and thanked my Friend upstairs, He just said "yore welcome, Frosty." Of course the feller settin' on top of the bull does his very best to hang on. But, should he, or I should say, *when* he gets throwed, a clown is real handy to give him a hand. One clown usually gets into a rubber barrel and thumbs his nose at the bull while the other feller gets down on his hands and knees and paws the ground like the bull does, to make him mad. Me, I'll take the barrel to hide in, how about you? This gives the rider a full second or so to climb the fence, if there's a fence handy, and he can make it in one jump. Otherwise, he stands a good chance of getting one

of those free rides to the edge of town where his friends stand around with their hats off. Should the rider get his hand caught in the riggin' when he gets throwed, a dozen cowboys will dash out and grab that 2,000 pounds of fightin' dynamite and crawl all over him to get the cowboy loose before he gets a hind hoof through his guts or his head smashed against the fence by a spinnin' bull. Bull ridin' is by far the most dangerous of all the rodeo events, but there are more cowboys a wantin' to show their guts or skill in bull ridin' than in any of the other events. So, I am pretty sure you won't fall asleep watchin' a bull ride. It's a long stretched-out eight seconds of hair-raisin' thrill such as you never had before.

BULL RIDING

Bull riders probably have the simplest set of rules to follow in this most dangerous event in rodeo. A Brahma, even though the name does sound a bit like a Hindu belly dancer, is far from being a lady. In fact the cowboy is atop up to a ton of twisting, pounding, sky-rocketing muscle, bone and guts. Whether the bull is a spinner or a high kicker, the cowboy knows that he is near putting his life on the line, or at least sticking his neck way out.

A Brahma bull's hide is very loose on his body, making it hard

Benny Reynolds   *(Photo by Ben Allen, Pasadena, California)*

for the cowboy to hang on. A rider once entered the arena carrying a hammer and a fist full of nails. When the judge asked him what the nails were for, he answered, "Why I aim tuh nail his hide down so's I'll know if I'm settin' on his back or hangin' on his belly."

Whether or not the cowboy manages to stay on the full eight seconds, he still has the job of getting out of the arena in one piece before those vicious horns can disembowel, cram his teeth down his gullet and probably tromp on him besides. The only other man in the arena is the colorful clown or clowns who are always willing to risk their lives when necessary to lure the bull from the fallen rider.

Each of the two judges score the cowboy and the bull separately, from 1 to 25 points for the rider, and the bull easily earns himself another 1 to 25 points for his own humble effort. Unlike other riding events, the bull rider does not have to spur his bull, which is just as well, as he is kept fairly busy just trying to keep his seat, let alone having other chores to look after.

The rider will be disqualified if bucked off, touching equipment or his person or bull, using sharp spurs, or placing spurs or edge of chaps under the rope when rope is being tightened.

BAREBACK RIDING

Regulation bareback riding rigging is a flat piece of leather with a hand hold fastened on with a cinch around the bronc's belly. Nothin' to set on except the bronc's bare back. No stirrups to absorb the jolts from the stiff-legged leaps, no buck-rein to help keep his balance. The cowboy gets a zero if his spurs are not over the shoulders of the bronc when the bronc's feet hit the ground on the first leap out of the chute.

Extra credit is given for spurring over the shoulders but the cowboy's legs are usually "waving in the air like a migratin' bullfrog" and he can't get his legs down that far. All it takes is eight seconds to win. After the first few seconds, the cowboy is probably numb all over and don't know or give a damn if he has been ridin' eight seconds or eight minutes.

Each of two judges score cowboy and bronc separately from 1 to 25 points. All four figures added together could equal 100, which is rarely if ever reached.

And all this time the cowboy must have one hand in the air. Did you ever try neckin' yore gal with one hand high in the air? Kind of slows a gent up some, don't yuh think?

DALLY TEAM ROPING
Sean Pascoe and Tootie Hudson

(Photo: Louise L. Serpa,
Courtesy Tucson Chamber of Commerce)

DALLY TEAM ROPING

This is the only event in which two cowboys compete as a team in the actual roping of the animal. As with calf roping, this is a rapid-fire operation. No tied ropes are permitted. As the animal is caught, each cowboy must dally his rope (snubbed with a turn or two around saddle horn and held in that manner).

One cowboy ropes the steer around the horns or neck and then turns his horse back sharply to the left giving the "heeler" a chance to rope both hind feet below the hocks. If only one hind foot is caught the team is fined five seconds.

The "head" cowboy must catch the steer around both horns, around the neck or half a head (head and one horn). Both ropers must then back away from the standing steer until horses and riders are facing the steer and ropes are stretched fairly tight.

There are two timers—a barrier judge and a field flag judge. Time is taken between the two flags. Maximum weight of the steer shall be around 700 pounds. A dropped or broken rope will be considered as no time.

SADDLE BRONC RIDING

Saddle bronc riding has always been the classic event of rodeos. Eight seconds of vicious violence - much less if the bronc wins. Setting on the hurricane deck of a rough one you will probably think you have split at the crotch, your liver turned over, your eyeballs bulge as you near enter a coma waiting for the ground to come up so you can "eat dirt without stoopin'."

By this time, you are ready to welcome the loving arms of the pickup man and hit ground, grin sheepishly at the cheering crowd, pick up yore hat and with one hand holding yore rump, limp painfully from the arena. Should you ask the cowboy how he enjoyed the ride he will probably admit to "having aches in a lot of new places," and that "quite a few nuts an' bolts have been loosened."

All broncs are furnished by the stock contractor and each cowboy's bronc is selected by a judge drawing a number out of a hat. Big broncs are the choice of the cowboys, as a large horse is more powerful and can usually put up a better fight.

Spurring is a must and plays a large part in the scoring of the judges. Rider is required to have his spurs high in the base of the bronc's neck and hold them there until the bronc's front feet hit the ground outside the chute. If he doesn't spur his bronc out of the chute, his ride is forfeited. Saddles are usually furnished by the stock contractor or by the rider if they meet strict specifications.

Cowboys must hold one hand in the air with the other holding the buck-rein. Rider can be disqualified for pulling leather, changing hands on rein, wrapping rein around hand, losing stirrup or touching animal or equipment with free hand. Each judge scores cowboy and bronc separately from 1 to 25 points. All four figures added together could equal 100, seldom if ever reached.

CALF ROPING

Lightning-fast teamwork between man and horse is necessary to win in calf roping. When the barrier goes down, the calf "takes off like a cut cat" with the horse leaping out after it.

A neck catch and the horse near buries his tail in the ground in a sudden stop, as the rider fades from the horse, runs down the rope, throws the calf and ties up three wildly kicking legs. What a thrill it is to watch the horse as he breaks into a dead run on the first jump, follows the calf in just the right position for the rider to make his throw, slides to a stop when the calf is caught, backs if necessary to keep the rope tight while the rider is going down the rope, throws the calf and makes the tie.

If the calf is jerked down when caught, it must be allowed to get to its feet before being thrown for the tie. The calf may be tied by crossing any three legs and the tie must hold for six seconds.

Calf roping is the smoothest and fastest action of all arena events. Calves weigh 200 to 350 pounds, depending on breed. It takes a good horse to cut even a second from the chute to the cowboy's throw.

As the horse's tail hits the ground, so does the cowboy, and he is halfway down the rope before the calf hits the end. Notice the apparent ease with which the cowboy lifts that two or three hundred pounds of fighting and bellerin' son of a catamount with one hand in the flank and the other grabbin' a handful of hair and slams it to the ground. In less than a second he has slipped the loop of the six foot piggin' string carried between his teeth, over the top front leg, pulled up the two kickin' hind legs, made a couple of turns and a half-hitch and raised his arms that the job is done.

Most folks in the settin' stands don't even get their eyes focused before the job is done.

STEER WRESTLING

As in calf roping, the steer gets a head start down the arena with the "dogger" on one side and his "hazer" on the other to keep the steer running straight. At the right split second the "dogger" drops out of the saddle onto the head of the steer and digs in his boot heels to slow him up as he tries to twist him down.

Sounds easy, but it's about "as dangerous as kickin' a loaded polecat." A flick of the steer's head could poke a long horn into yore eye "quickern' an old maid can crawl under a bed." Nope, when I want to tango, it won't be with a half-ton steer.

When the steer is flat on its side with all four feet and head straight, time is taken. If the steer goes down the wrong way, the cowboy must let him up and try again. Should the steer get loose after he is jumped on, the cowboy can take only one step to regain his hold. But, before the cowboy can take that step, the steer is usually long gone.

BARREL RACING
Connie Kaufman

(Photo: Louise L. Serpa
Courtesy Tucson Chamber of Commerce)

BARREL RACING

Barrel racing has reached a high level of popularity with rodeo fans throughout the country. Early day rodeos featured the lady-girls in bronc riding, relay racing, trick and fancy riding, etc., but present day rodeos have pretty much settled on barrel racing as their main contribution to the rodeo game.

Three barrels are set in a triangle and the rider must circle the barrels against time. A judge drops a flag as the rider starts the run and again as she comes back across the line. If the horse and rider knock over a barrel, they will be penalized five seconds. This of course makes it almost impossible to turn in a good time. Only highly-bred fast horses stand any chance in this fast action event.

While riders don't exactly have to be highly-bred, they do have to be darn good riders to hang on during the hairpin turns so sharp that at times a stirrup will nearly touch the ground. As the rider makes the last turn and heads for home with her quirt playing a tattoo on the side of her bronc, she certainly gets the encouragement from the folks up in the settin' seats.

RODEO COWBOY
ALL-AROUND CHAMPIONS

Year	Cowboy	Money Won
1959	Jim Shoulders, Henryetta, OK	$ 32,905
1960	Harry Tompkins, Dublin, TX	32,532
1961	Benny Reynolds, Melrose, MT	31,309
1962	Tom Nesmith, Bethel, OK	32,511
1963	Dean Oliver, Boise, ID	31,329
1964	Dean Oliver, Boise, ID	31,150
1965	Dean Oliver, Boise, ID	33,163
1966	Larry Mahan, Brooks, OR	40,358
1967	Larry Mahan, Brooks, OR	51,996
1968	Larry Mahan, Salem, OR	49,129
1969	Larry Mahan, Brooks, OR	57,726
1970	Larry Mahan, Brooks, OR	41,493
1971	Phil Lyne, George West, TX	49,245
1972	Phil Lyne, Georeg West, TX	60,852
1973	Larry Mahan, Dallas, TX	64,447
1974	Tom Ferguson, Miami, OK	66,929
1975	Tom Ferguson, Miami, OK	50,300
1976	Tom Ferguson, Miami, OK	87,908
1977	Tom Ferguson, Miami, OK	76,730
1978	Tom Ferguson, Miami, OK	103,734
1979	Tom Ferguson, Miami, OK	96,272
1980	Paul Tierney, Rapid City, SD	105,568
1981	Jimmie Cooper, Monument, NM	105,861
1982	Chris Lybbert, Coyote, CA	123,709
1983	Roy Cooper, Durant, OK	153,391
1984	Dee Pickett, Caldwell, ID	122,618

BOBWIRE

There was a time when there was probably around fifty or sixty million buffalo scattered over the western plains. For centuries the Indians had depended on them for their main livelihood. Then came the white man. He, too, lived high on the hog, 'er I mean buffalo, as did the Indians, but instead of utilizing the entire buffalo, he would shoot a half-to-three-quarter-ton buffalo, cut out its tongue and a piece of hump and leave the carcass for the coyotes.

Soon the government figured there was too much good land going to waste, and with buffalo hides in big demand for robes, garments and dozens of other uses, hordes of hide hunters soon whittled the buffalo down to near extinction. After the wolves and other meat-eating varmints had cleaned up on the meat, a few years later came the bone crew.

Buffalo bones were knee-deep in spots. Shipped to eastern markets, they were ground up for fertilizer and other uses.

When the Indians saw their buffalo meat and tepee-building buffalo hides being rapidly eliminated, they decided to do a little killing on their own. Quite a few skirmishes took place between ther and whites.

They soon managed to get holt of some rifles, and with a little fire-water, they managed to put up quite a fight. The whites, of course, won and soon had them penned up on reservations.

Land was now free for the taking, whether a few acres to build a sod shack on, or a chunk sixty or a hundred miles on a side, where a man could run up to 50,000 head or more. The big ranchers pretty much had the run of the country until small ranchers, and later on, homesteaders, moved in.

To get a start, these little ranchers would slap their brand on the near endless number of calves called mavericks, maverick being a calf running around without a Ma, or whose Ma sported a different brand.

Of course, the small rancher also had to have a share of good graze and a few waterholes. This caused some bickering back and forth between the big ranchers and the little ranchers, nesters, homesteaders or whatever you want to call them. But these feuds were usually settled with a little playful shootin' back and forth. Or maybe as a result of a friendly visit by the big rancher, the nester could easily be convinced that it might be better for his health if he would move back to Minnesota, if that's where he came from. Either that, or he always had the option of taking up permanent residence on the side of the hill overlooking where his shack used to set before it caught fire one night and burned to the

"SCUTT'S CLIP"

PAT. BY H. B. SCUTT JUNE 18, 1878

J. BROTHERTON ROUND BARB

PAT. SEPT. 3, 1887

WORMLEY "Y" BARB THREE LINE
PATENTED BY ABRAM V. WORMLEY
NOVEMBER 2, 1875

"SCUTT'S H PLATE"
SAME AS "CLIP" PAT.

T. V. ALLIS
BARBLESS RIBBON AND SINGLE WIRE
PATENTED JULY 26, 1881

WATKIN'S "LAZY PLATE"
PAT. BY WILLIAM WATKINS NOV. 21, 1876

GLIDDEN HERRINGBONE
PATENTED BY J. F. GLIDDEN, AUGUST 22, 1876

GLIDDEN BARELY BARB
(SHARP POINT OF BARB ALL THAT IS OUT)
PAT. NOV. 24, 1874

GLIDDEN THREE LINE BAR WIRE
(TWO LINES DIFFERENT GAUGE WITH SMALL
HIGH TINSEL BAR TWISTED IN TOGETHER)
PAT. NOV. 24, 1874

A. J. UPHAMS TWO LINE "SNAIL BARB"

PAT. SEPT. 4, 1883

D. C. STOVER, PATENTED JUNE 29, 1875
COMMONLY CALLED "CORSICANA CLIP"

GLIDDEN HOG WIRE, GALV. LINE
RUSTY EXTRA LONG BARBS.
PAT. J. F. GLIDDEN, NOV. 24, 1874

MERRILL'S EARLY FOUR POINT
PAT. BY L & J MERRILL SEPT. 29, 1871

A. C. DECKER'S SPREAD

PAT. JUNE 3, 1884

BAKER AND GLIDDEN TWO LINE
BAKER BARB ON ONE LINE, GLIDDEN
BARB ON OTHER LINE

JAN. 22, 1878   **CAREY'S MACHINE PATENT**
"GREENBRIAR" OR "WRAP AROUND"
JOHN HOLLNER, ITHICA, NEB.

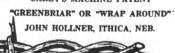

PAT. J. BROTHERTON, SEPT. 3, 1887
FORKED TONGUE BROTHERTON BARB

L. P. JUDSON NOTCHED RIBBON
PAT. AUG. 15, 1871

ground.

Then along came the Homestead Act. Anybody could file on 160 acres of land, build himself an 8-by-10, or if married, maybe a 10-by-12-foot log, dugout or sod shack. By living on it five years, or at least make believe he had, and if still alive by the end of that time, he could prove up on it. Or he could live on it six months and commute by paying the government $125 and get title to his homestead. Girls and women were plenty scarce in those days, but once in a while a feller might be lucky and rope himself a country school-marm or maybe a mail order wife who might turn out to be a pretty good cook, too.

Of course a big rancher didn't like it when a homesteader moved in and staked himself 160 acres smack-dab in the middle of a choice meadow with a spring-fed waterhole. After a time, homesteading got to the point that the big ranchers realized that if they were going to survive, they would near have to own the land to keep control of their graze. So, if a big rancher had 30 cowboys, he would have each of them file on 160 acres, pay their commuting charge at the end of six months and have the cowboys deed the land to the ranch in exchange for a promise to be kept on the payroll, at least 'til after the fall roundup. Nor was it uncommon for the rancher himself to sign up for maybe a couple dozen or more cowboys who might have worked on the ranch for a month or so, ten years ago.

Big cattle outfits saw the handwriting on the wall and even talked some of building fenced-in lanes across the cattle country, so they could still trail their big drives of cattle from range to market.

Then, to further heckle the ranchers, some feller thought up the bright idea of a wire fence with barbs on it to keep critters out of his wife's garden. The fence idea kept growing and ranchers soon learned that if a bobwire fence could keep critters out, why wouldn't it keep critters in? Soon everybody started building fences.

By nosing around I found that the earliest bobwire fences were patented around 1853. I mean fences with barbs on the wire, not just a plain piece of wire nailed to a tree. Records show that a feller name of Joseph F. Glidden got his patent on bobwire on October 27, 1873, and has since been known as the "father of bobwire"! As for me, he can have the honor, as who in his right mind would want to be the father of a roll of bobwire? The same feller also invented wire-stretchers and the wooden spools on which wire was wrapped so you could string the wire from post to post if you wanted to build a fence.

GLIDDEN ALL ALUMINUM WIRE
PAT. NOV. 24, 1874

WILKES TWO LINE
WITH BARB ON ONE LINE
PATENTED E. V. WILKES, JUNE 17, 1879

GLIDDEN BARB ON BOTH LINES
(ALTERNATE LONG AND SHORT BARBS)
PAT. NOV. 24, 1874

J. GLIDDENS' THREE STRAND CABLE WIRI
PAT. FEB. 8, 1876, BARB ON LARGE LINE WIRE

GLIDDEN FOUR LINE
(THREE SMALL, ONE LARGE WITH BARB)
PATENTED NOVEMBER 24, 1874

BROTHERTON 2¼ INCH BETWEEN BARB

"HOG WIRE"   PAT. SEPT. 3, 1878

GLIDDEN BARB ON BOTH LINES . . .
SPACED ONE INCH APART
PAT. NOV. 24, 1874

MODERN WIRE
DODGE & WASHBURN TYPE HALF ROUND BARB
PAT. JAN. 4, 1872

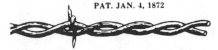

A. J. UPHAM STAPLE BARB ON TWO LINES
PAT. AUG. 29, 1876

GLIDDEN TWO LINE GOAT BARB
(LINES ARE TWO DIFFERENT SIZES)
PAT. NOV. 24, 1874

JAYNE AND HILL TWO LINE ON ONE LINE
PATENTED APRIL 11, 1876

ONE AROUND TWO
                    NET WIRE

THREE LINE BROTHERTON WIRE
PAT. J. BROTHERTON, SEPT. 3, 1887

GLIDDEN'S REISSUE No. 6914
PAT. J. F. GLIDDEN, FEB. 8, 1876

KILMER'S "WINDOW" WIRE
PATENTED MAY 12, 1885

D. C. STOVER
PATENTED MAY 1, 1877

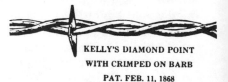

KELLY'S DIAMOND POINT
WITH CRIMPED ON BARB
PAT. FEB. 11, 1868

And, speakin' of rolls of bobwire, I recall when I was a lad around 12 years old, it more than once fell to my lot to help Pa or one of my older brothers string the wire for maybe a new hoss pasture or a line fence. Now, a bobwire spool is built just like a spool of thread like Ma used to have in her button box, along with pins an' needles an' buttons an' patches she used to keep our overalls lookin' good. An' you ought to see Ma mend socks. She could take a sock with a big hole in it and first sew up an' down on the hole, then sideways, and I'm telling you that hole would generally last longer than the rest of the sock.

Bobwire spools have a hole runnin' sideways through them. If we didn't have anything better handy, we would use a wagon-box endgate rod through the spool so a man on each end of it could walk down the line of post, lettin' the spool unwind.

As endgate rods were too small we would use a crowbar if one was available. Now in case you don't know what a crowbar is, I'll tell you, cause it's about the handiest tool you can have around your ranch or farm. And no, it wasn't made just to dig post holes with, cause you could use it for such as diggin', poundin', leverin', drivin' fence poles, moving a barn, pole-axin' a sick critter or just having it handy in case of an Indian attack.

Some folks would use just a common round bar of iron for a crowbar with the bottom end sharpened. Why, such a tool was about "as worthless as a pail of hot spit" to dig a posthole with.

The best made bars have a square shape from the point up to a foot or more up the bar. To use the bar to set a post you hold up the crowbar on end and sight it in with the posts you already set. Elsewise your fence will be about "as crooked as a dog's hind leg." Take a few jabs straight down into the dirt, say 6 or 8 inches, depending how hard the dirt is.

Then take a holt of the bar at the top and wind it around in circles in either direction. Now I don't mean to twist the bar with your hands. I mean just keep it moving around in a circle about 6 or 8 inches in diameter at top of bar.

The secret is that when a square corner of the bar digs into the side of the hole, it bites into the dirt until the next square takes a holt and so forth. By going round and round, the hole keeps getting a little bigger and works its way down making the hole deeper.

Sometimes if the dirt is kind of spongy and not too hard, why that old bar would go down near as fast as if you just dropped it into the hole.

Then all you got to do is take a sharpened post, shove it down the hole, give it a couple whacks with the bar, kick in some dirt, tromp on it with your size 14 boot-heel and maybe tamp it down

GLIDDEN FOUR LINE,
BARB AROUND TWO
PATENTED NOVEMBER 24, 1874

J. BRINKERHOFF

PAT. MAY 17, 1881

GLIDDEN BARB WITH TWO EXTRA

HEAVY AND SLIGHTLY OVAL LINE WIRES

PAT. J. F. GLIDDEN, NOV. 24, 1874

J. BRINKERHOFF TWISTED

PAT. APRIL 8, 1879

THREE LINE SPLICED INTO A TWO LINE WIRE

PAT. J. F. GLIDDEN, NOV. 24, 1874

UNION PACIFIC R. R. WIRE

ONE ROUND, ONE SQUARE LINE WIRE

PAT. J. F. GLIDDEN, NOV. 24, 1874

ENGLISH W.W. I ENTANGLEMENT WIRE
APPROXIMATELY 1916

TWO SQUARE LINE WIRE

PAT. J. F. GLIDDEN, NOV. 24, 1874

GLIDDEN SIX STRAND CABLE WIRE
PATENTED APRIL 16, 1886

E. SIMS, PATENTED MAY 30, 1876

SCUTT'S "ARROW PLATE"

SAME AS "CLIP" PAT.

E. V. WILKES "DOUBLE STAPLE" ON TWO LINES

PAT. JUNE 17, 1879

CATTLE RUSTLING

Brand Artist
Burnin' Rawhide
Brand Blotter
Calves Don't Suck
   the Right Cows
Careless With His
   Branding Iron
Carvin' Ears

His Cows
   Have Twins
Rides With an
   Extra Cinch Ring
Rope and
   Ring Man
Rustler
Sleepering
Slow Branding

Sticky Rope
Too Handy
   with a Rope
Usin' a Long Rope
Wet Branding
Working Ahead
   of the Roundup
Working Brands

with the end of the crowbar. Why, I'll bet I can go down to our old ranch and find some post that I stomped in 75 years ago.

But, what I want to say is that stringin' bobwire is about as ornery a job as you can find. As we walked along stringin' the wire, about every 10 feet or so the barbs would get stuck on each other and it took a he-man with a pair of bullhide gloves and a club to keep the wires unstuck so it would unroll evenly from the reel. When the wires were unstuck with the club, about 10 or 15 feet of wire would leap from the spool from the tension. And believe me, you better have your hands far away from the spool or the barbs would rake the hide off your hands and arms before you could spit and hollar howdy. And I haven't told you that a crowbar weighs probably 20 pounds or more. A spool of bobwire weighin' another 50 or 75 pounds hanging in the middle of the bar didn't exactly improve our temper none.

When I was barely able to climb up the side of a hoss, one of my jobs was to take a hammer an' a saddlebag of staples an' ride the fences to replace missing staples. Our hoss pasture was a mile square and in the spring and fall when the many coulees and cricks was loaded with prairie chickens and ducks, it didn't take any urgin' for brother Twit and me to "ride the hoss pasture." Instead of ridin', we'd grab a couple slices of bread with some watered-down sugar on top and a handful of dried prunes and spend the whole day replacin' maybe 3 or 4 staples. Course we didn't tell Pa that, and I'll bet you wouldn't have either, would you?

I've just give you a lot of know-how on what bobwire is an' how to make a fence with it. Now, I'll bet you will be flabbergasted when I tell you there are at least 898 different kinds of bobwire or wire close enough to be called bobwire. If you don't believe this, a feller down in Texas actually sent me a book that he had published that even shows a picture of all the different wires along with the name of the gent that thought them up and the date patented.

Should you want one of the books, just write to Jack Glover, care of Cow Puddle Press, Sunset, Texas 76270. Following are fifty or so of the brands, taken at random from Jack's book, showing the almost impossible variety of the different wires. Thanks to you, Jack.

What is it, a handkerchief, neckerchief, bandanna, wipe or what???

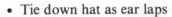

Once a feller asked me why a cowpoke always wore a red or colored bandanna around his neck. So I told him what for, such as . . .

- Tie down hat as ear laps
- Face mask - for homely fellers
- Pull over nose when cold
- Table cloth - on the trail
- Napkin for under yore chin
- Carry water to yore hoss
- Clean yore sixshooter with
- Face towel - to wipe yore face with
- Wrap yore leg if yore boot chafes yuh
- To protect back of neck from sun, bugs

- Makeshift for handkerchief
- Spread on water to drink through
- Tie up a sore hand or leg
- Keep mosquitoes away
- Rinse out horse's mouth
- Toilet paper in a pinch
- Leave on a bush for a sign
- Write a note or letter on
- Wrap up a little animal, maybe
- Start a fire with in a pinch
- As a belt around yore belly
- Hang under Stetson as a sun shade
- Feed oats to yore hoss in
- As a compress for a wound
- Hogtie a critter with it

- Use as pants if you wet yours
- Wave as a signal
- As a hackamore
- Wrap up a lunch, if you got one
- Wash cloth - should yuh ever wash
- To set in the sand on
- A makeshift piggin' string
- Catch rain water to drink
- Tote firewood in
- Keep mosquitoes or bugs out of nose
- For yore gal friend to set on - or yore lap
- Carry mud to chink yore shack
- Stake out a sand turtle
- Gather wild fruit in
- Tie a calf on yore saddle
- For a screen on yore shack window
- Tie a splint on a broke arm or leg
- Hold your hot spider (frypan) over fire
- Dish rag - to go along with yore towel
- Wipe yore nose on, even
- Use for mittens on a cold day
- Net to catch a fish in
- Mask if holding up a bank
- Rabbit snare - case yuh are real hungry
- To play "old woman" with a poke bonnet
- Tote cowchips - better than in yore pocket
- Charlie Russell used his to paint on
- As a broke spur strap
- Wrap up a chunk of venison - after you get it
- Shine up yore boots
- Dish towel - different from face towel
- They make good hip-pocket insurance.

Well, at least I gave the feller a few things a neckerchief is handy for.

WHISKEY - you name it!

Alcohol
Barleycorn
Base Burner
Bouse
Boose
Brandy
Brave Maker
Bug Juice
Coffin Varnish
Conversation Fluid
Corn Squeezings
Drink
Fire Water
Gin

Grog
Gut Warmer
Home Brew
Hooch
Hooker
Liquor
Liquid Dynamite
Liquid Fire
Moonshine
Neck Oil
Nose Paint
Panther Piss
Pot

Pottle
Red Eye
Rot Gut
Rum
Spirits
Scamper Juice
Snake Poison
Snort
Swill
Tarantula Juice
Tonsil Varnish
Schnapps
Whiskey
Wild Mare Juice

KILLING

Bed him down
Bit the dust
Blotted him out
Blow out his lamp
Bucked out
Bumped off
Bushwhacked
Cooked his goose
Crawled his hump
Croaked him
Curled him up
Cut him down
Did him in
Dry gulched him
Dabbled in gore
Downed him
Finished him off
Fed him a fatal pill
Gave him a free ride
He played his last card
Hung up his hide
Gunned him down

Kicked the bucket
Killed him dead
Knocked him cold
Knocked him off
Landed in a shallow grave
Laid him out cold
Made wolf meat of him
Meat-axed him
Mowed him down
Murdered him
Put a window in his skull
Put him away
Put him on ice
Put him out of his misery
Put him to sleep
Rubbed him out
Settled his hash
Smoked him out
Stopped his clock
Snuffed him out
Took him for a ride
Wiped him out
Wore him plumb down

Meet the Illustrator
RON SCOFIELD

As a boy on a homestead in southern Oregon, Ron Scofield heard his father and grandfather tell many stories of cowboys, Indians and pioneers and the rich history of the Rogue River area. As soon as he could hold a pencil, Ron started drawings of those colorful times. Today, his passion for the Old West lives on. Ron's paintings, drawings and carvings adorn the walls of houses and galleries throughout the West.

Ron, his wife Marie and son Tom live on Red Mule Ranch in the old goldrush town of Fiddletown, California, where Ron builds and restores wagons and carriages for museums and private collectors— one more way to live close to the Old West.

In 1976, Ron and family traveled across the United States by covered wagon pulled by two mules, Jim and John. Following the legendary Santa Fe Trail, the trip took six months, giving Ron a deep appreciation for the strength of the American pioneer.

Ron's paintings and drawings have captured for eternity the laughter of the jolly cowboy, the majesty and beauty of the American Indian.

The rumble of covered wagons of early pioneer times still echoes across the hills and valleys of the Red Mule Ranch. The Old West lives on!

Meet the Author
EDGAR R. "FROSTY" POTTER

"Frosty," as he likes to be called, says that since just a button on the Diamond N Ranch in North Dakota even his own Ma called him Frosty.

He first saw the light of day in 1895. Their cattle ranch was just across the Cannonball River from the Sioux Indian Reservation. His Pa claims he cut his first eye-teeth by chewing on the barrel of a .45 Colt.

A trail from Mandan ran right through the ranch and the Indians pitched their tepees on a hillside spot that the ranch had provided for their use. Usually the buck sat on the wagon seat with the squaw and papoose sitting looking backward on the wagon box floor behind the seat, along with the tepee poles and a buffalo hide or a canvas tepee covering.

Each wagon outfit usually had an Indian digger (small horse) tied to a hame for trading stock and, of course, three or four dogs. Frosty says the family was usually well supplied with hand-beaded moccasins, with some sharp trading of maybe two pair of moccasins for a fair-to-middlin'-size dog.

So, with ponies at the discount rate of two or three dogs per horse, the small-fry early in life usually had their own string of broncs. In later years the Diamond N really got on the map when Potter talked the post office into having a mail route and a post office which was named Diamond, North Dakota, after the ranch.

Ranching was hard and cruel and a man was often hard put to keep the wolf from the door. As Frosty says, drought, blizzards, rustling and just plain hard luck could easily whittle a man down to sowbelly and beans, that is, if he could scare up a few beans and substitute a neighbor's calf for the sowbelly.

Slang those days was as common as tumbleweeds and a cowpuncher was about "as helpless as a dummy with his hands cut off" without his colorful language or when "setting on his heels drawing word pictures in the dirt like a chicken scratching in a dung heap."

Frosty's revised *Cowboy Slang* book now has an outstanding collection of around 2,000 cowboy slang phrases collected over a period of some 70 years of western living. His stories of brands, bobwire, cattle rustling, cattle and horses are written as only Frosty knows how, with his own brand of humor thrown in.

Frosty hung up his saddle quite a few years back after living for 35 years in the beautiful Bitteroot Valley in western Montana. He has worked with law people and at one time trained police and sheriff's men in marksmanship and the handling of firearms. He still hand-loads his own ammunition for his several guns, including his old .45 Colt that he has had for over sixty years. His deputy sheriff badge is among his valued possessions. Always the hunter, he has taken his share of deer, elk, moose, antelope, bear and a few mountain goat. He now admits the animals don't cooperate any more—he can't get up to where they are, and they won't come down to where he is!

With his wife, Eileen, he now lives in another famous ranching country where Indian fighting, cattle rustling and wars are still topics of conversation. Payson, Arizona is the third healthiest spot in the whole world!!!!! and is known nationwide as the only town having had a rodeo for 100 consecutive years.

Yes, Frosty likes his salty talk and can hold his own when it comes to dishing it out. His motto is "don't never interfere with nothing what don't bother yuh none." Ask for the state of his health and his reply is usually "well, like a dead hoss, I ain't kickin'."

Books from Golden West Publishers

Read of the daring deeds and exploits of Wyatt Earp, Buckey O'Neill, the Rough Riders, Arizona Rangers, cowboys, Power brothers shootout, notorious Tom Horn, Pleasant Valley wars, "first" American revolution—action-packed true tales of early Arizona! *Arizona Adventure (by Marshall Trimble), 160 pages . . . $5.00.*

The lost hopes, the lost lives—the lost gold! Facts, myths and legends of the Lost Dutchman Gold Mine and the Superstition Mountains. Told by a geologist who was there! *Fools' Gold (by Robert Sikorsky), 144 pages . . . $5.00.*

Take the back roads to and thru Arizona's natural wonders—Canyon de Chelly, Wonderland of Rocks, Monument Valley, Rainbow Bridge, Four Peaks, Swift Trail, Alamo Lake, Virgin River Gorge, Palm Canyon, Red Rock Country! *Arizona—off the beaten path! (by Thelma Heatwole), 144 pages . . . $4.50.*

Plants, animals, rocks, minerals, geologic history, natural environments, landforms, resources, national forests and outdoor survival—with maps, photographs, drawings, charts, index. *Arizona Outdoor Guide (by Ernest E. Snyder), 126 pages . . . $5.00*

Visit the silver cities of Arizona's golden past with this prize-winning reporter-photographer. Come along to the towns whose heydays were once wild and wicked! See crumbling adobe walls, old mines, cemeteries, cabins and castles. *Ghost Towns and Historical Haunts in Arizona (by Thelma Heatwole), 144 pages . . . $4.50.*

Arizona Museums—See them all! More than 175 fascinating museums, zoos, botanical gardens and art centers are described and photographed in this up-do-date volume, complete with maps. *Arizona Museums (by Al and Mildred Fischer), 88 large pages . . . $5.00.*

Books from Golden West Publishers

Southwestern frontier tales more thrilling than fiction. Trimble makes history come alive with humor, pathos and irony of pioneer lives. First train sneaks into Arizona, sheriff captures gang by auto, railroads pay millions to land "baron," etc. *In Old Arizona (by Marshall Trimble), 160 pages . . . $5.00.*

A taste of the Old Southwest, from sizzling Indian fry bread to prickly pear marmalade, from spicy pinto beans to outdoor barbecuing. *Arizona Cook Book (by Al and Mildred Fischer), 144 pages . . . $3.50.*

Get acquainted with the California lifestyle via these recipes for Spanish and Mexican dishes, wine treats, avocados, dates, citrus, figs, nuts, salads and ocean foods. *California Favorites Cook Book (by Al and Mildred Fischer), 144 pages . . . $3.50.*

Tempting recipes for luscious pies, dazzling desserts, sunshine salads, novelty meat and seafood dishes, and tangy thirst-quenchers with oranges, grapefruit, lemons, tangerines, etc. *Citrus Recipes from the Citrus Belt (by Al and Mildred Fischer), 128 pages . . . $3.50.*

Now, you can prepare these favorite recipes— tacos, tamales, menudo, enchiladas, burros, salsas, frijoles, huevos, almendrado. Home style! Delicious! *Mexican Family Favorites Cook Book (by Maria Teresa Bermudez), 144 pages . . . $5.00.*

Two cookbooks in one—the best of chili cookery, from mild to fiery, with and without beans—and a variety of taste-tempting foods made with chile peppers. *Chili-Lovers' Cook Book (by Al and Mildred Fischer), 128 pages . . . $3.50.*

Order from your book dealer or direct from publisher.

■■■■■■■■■■■■■ **ORDER BLANK** ■■■■■■

TREASURES IN GOLD
Post Office Box 1661
Apple Valley, CA 92307

Publishers

Please ship the following books:

⌐...... Arizona Adventure ($5.00)

...... Arizona Cook Book ($3.50)

...... Arizona Museums ($5.00)

...... Arizona—Off the Beaten Path ($4.50)

...... Arizona Outdoor Guide ($5.00)

...... California Favorites ($3.50)

...... Chili-Lovers' Cook Book ($3.50)

...... Citrus Recipes ($3.50)

...... Cowboy Slang ($5.00)

...... Fools' Gold (Lost Dutchman Mine) ($5.00)

...... Ghost Towns in Arizona ($4.50)

...... Greater Phoenix Street Maps Book ($4.00)

...... How to Succeed in Selling Real Estate ($3.50)

...... In Old Arizona ($5.00)

...... Mexican Cook Book ($5.00)

I enclose $ _____ (including $1 per order postage, handling).

Name _____

Address _____

City _____ State _____ Zip_____

This order blank may be photo copied